The Art of
Significant
RELATIONSHIPS

The Art of
Significant
RELATIONSHIPS

Chad Hymas   Dan Clark   Devin D. Thorpe

**with
14 contributing
authors**

The Art of Significant Relationships

ISBN-13: 9781630729011

About this Anthology

THIS ANTHOLOGY WAS created by the National Speakers Association Mountain West Chapter on behalf of the authors in this book. Only members of the chapter who met the rigorous standards for membership in the National Speakers Association were invited to participate.

The NSA Mountain West Chapter includes some of the best speakers in the country, including Hall of Fame speakers Dan Clark and Chad Hymas who both participated in this book, along with fifteen other speakers.

The National Speakers Association is the premiere organization for professional speakers. Since its founding in 1973, thousands of speakers have joined to receive training and mentoring to reach the pinnacle of the speaking profession.

Acknowledgements

THIS ANTHOLOGY HAS been a team effort led by a committee comprising Tannen Ellis-Graham, Dr. Russell Gaede and Devin Thorpe. The team worked long hours to gather drafts, coordinate edits, commission cover art and publish the book.

Jae Dansie edited the manuscript helping all of our authors to look their best.

Dr. Jay Polmar designed the covers.

Jimmy Sevilleno formatted the interior of the book for print and digital publication.

Dan Clark, the Hall of Fame speaker and bestselling author, was the visionary who conceived of this project, without whom it certainly would not exist and to whom the authors wish to express a special debt of gratitude.

Chad Hymas, also a Hall of Fame speaker and bestselling author, lent his substantial credibility to the project as well. His participation helped to make this book a compelling product.

Of course, we the authors are ultimately responsible for the content of the book, including its conclusions, recommendation and errors.

A. Kent Merrell, Becky Mackintosh, Brandon Kelly, Chad Hymas, Colleen Cook, Dan Clark, Darren Johansen, Devin Thorpe, Karen Lindsay, Leta Greene, Martin Hurlburt, Michelle McCullough, Mitchel Seehusen, Paul Jenkins, Russell Gaede, Sydne Jacques, and Tannen Ellis-Graham.

Table of Contents

Leadership and Love Unfeigned

by A. Kent Merrell

ARNOLD R. KNAPP, while Vice President of Steiner American Corporation, in a presentation about leadership to an audience of college students said,

> "Over a hundred years ago a great religious leader gave us a guide for all who have authority or control over individuals. This religious leader said, 'No power or influence can or ought to be maintained by virtue of office alone, only by persuasion, by long-suffering, by gentleness and meekness, and by love unfeigned; by kindness, and pure knowledge, which shall greatly enlarge the soul without hypocrisy, and without guile.'"

Mr. Knapp went on to share how this had affected and guided many of his fellow leaders as they presided over great organizations. I have reflected on the inspiration of that religious leader many times as I have tried to study and understand the entire leadership landscape. Long before the plethora of modern-day speeches, articles, and books written and presented about generating, maintaining, and exercising influence, this leader laid out the true source of influence. A source which few leadership experts explore – Love Unfeigned.

Most of the effective leadership takes place in the quiet of a home, a small office, a company boardroom, a community council room, and even on the playground. Yet the leadership we see and study is usually found on the grand stage, in view of the world's media. Though I've never been invited to that grand stage where I've landed a plane on the Hudson River, rescued people from their houses in a hurricane, orchestrated the rescue of an Apollo spacecraft, or even united a nation against a common foe, I have experienced being led by loving leaders.

Let me briefly share a few personal examples along with a couple "grand stage" examples where Love Unfeigned was the foundation of true leadership.

Love Unfeigned at Home

As a young boy I used to get up in the morning to find my father studying, working, or praying in his small office which was directly across the hall from my bedroom. Many a time I would find my way across the hall to ask the great question, "Whatcha doing, Dad?" and we would talk. I can't begin to remember all the subjects we discussed, but the few I do remember are still lessons that have shaped my life. He not only taught these lessons verbally in the early hours of the day – he lived them all day. I won't rehearse them here, but years later, more than 40 years later, I run into people who share with me a life lesson they learned from my father. With deep sincerity, they share how this act or these words of instruction or encouragement made all the difference in their lives. He was not a man of any official authority or worldly consequence to have any wide popularity. Yet, his world mourned when he passed away. It was reported that the funeral procession traveling between the church chapel and the cemetery was nearly two miles long. He mentored and cared for everyone he met and they returned that respect and love.

It's one thing to be personal and to love as a leader when you are one-on-one or in a small group, but it becomes a different thing when you lead a large organization, a company, association, or nation. Yet a true leader can do so.

Love is best demonstrated within these large operations when you first love those around you personally, and then you love the organization and love what it stands for. You demonstrate that love, by showing respect to its principles and the efforts of those you lead in that organization.

Love Unfeigned in the Operating Room

Just as you show love to people individually by serving them, honoring them, respecting them, and knowing them, you do the same with a large group – it requires personal integrity, loyalty to the cause, to the sacrifice, and talents of the members of the group. It demands consistency of what you say and how you act in private and in public. After Pediatric Neurosurgeon Ben Carson's famous separation of the Binder twins, where Dr. Carson had assembled a team of over 70 specialists to help successfully separate the conjoined twins, Dr. Carson was one of the last to take any credit for the historic event. He loved his team and gave them the credit they deserved.

People will see your sacrifices, your passion, and your service. It's hard to serve in anonymity. Do it anyway. When you do it to be seen, you'll be seen through. It's the love, sacrifice, and true dedication in private that will be seen in the way you look, talk, walk, and the way you sincerely treat the organization, its principles and its people.

Love Unfeigned on the Ball Field

I recently had the fortunate opportunity of asking former Denver Broncos Captain and All-Pro Linebacker Karl Mecklenburg "what made the leader of a team like the Denver Broncos, the leader of the Denver Broncos?" Karl, who is still considered one of the NFL's most versatile players, and whose pro career included six Pro Bowl and three Super Bowl appearances, was as I mentioned, the captain of the team.

Karl told me that the real leader of the team was Hall of Fame quarterback John Elway. "In the cafeteria," Karl said, "Rather than sit with the big name players, John would sit at different tables each time. He got to know all the players, learned about their wives, their children, their lives, and he cared about them, he loved them. And they knew it. They gave it their all for him."

Karl continued, "Returning home from my last game before retiring, John and I were in the back of the plane talking and John told me he had to keep going until he got these men back to the Super Bowl. They deserved to be Super Bowl champs. He sincerely wanted them to win." The way Karl talked about John Elway demonstrated his love for John and John's love for his fellow team members.

Love Unfeigned in a Disaster Zone

How does love fit in when you are in a crisis leadership situation? There's not much time to build personal relationships where love develops and is expressed. Here is one such example. While sitting at home with his wife, Admiral Thad Allen, retired three-star Admiral of the US Coast Guard was among the millions of Americans watching on television the chaos caused by Hurricane Katrina in the Gulf. As he and the country watched floating bodies, flooded homes, despondent families, and lawlessness gripping the city of New Orleans, his mortification turned to anger. Speaking to other Coast Guard officers he asked "why wasn't somebody down there being the face of the federal government, standing in front of the Superdome, talking to CNN?"

A week later that is exactly what he was doing. He had been appointed deputy to Federal Emergency Management Agency (FEMA) director Michael D. Brown. That appointment put him in charge of the Hurricane Katrina search and rescue and recovery efforts in the Gulf. His assignment was, as he says, "Just get to New Orleans and figure out what's going on. Stabilize the situation."

Within a week President Bush realized that Admiral Allen was exactly who was needed and he was put in charge of the entire federal response, replacing the much-criticized Mike Brown. So in that kind of situation, where the thousands of people you are called upon to lead are in chaos, are discouraged, are being impaled by the media's criticism, and have no direction, how do you establish a relationship of love and caring?

Admiral Allen called an immediate all-hands meeting where he brought all the people he could gather together in the largest room he could find. Allen said,

> "I walked into that room and I looked around, and what I saw was 2,500 that were almost dragging on the ground. I jumped up on a desk and grabbed a megaphone and said I'm going to give you an order, **this is an order!** You are to treat everybody that you come in contact with that's been impacted by this storm as if they were a member of your family – your mother, your father, your brother, your sister. That's what I want you to do. And if you do that, two things will happen: Number one, if you make a mistake, you will probably err on the side of doing too much. And number two, if anybody has problem with what you did, they're problem is with me, not you."

At that point it's reported there was an audible collective sigh of relief and many began to weep. Admiral Allen told them what was important, what was valued, what their roles should be, and that their boss was behind them. He made the situation personal. He connected with thousands of people he didn't know and likely wouldn't know personally, but they knew he cared about them. Love happens when you know people care.

Love and caring can be demonstrated in countless ways – both in praise and in correction.

As a corporate leader, how do you care about people and love them without weakening your position of strength as their leader? What if you have to chasten them or correct them when you have become too personal? First it's important to dispel within yourself, a most common misconception, that caring about people and correcting them are incompatible. A leader—any leader, whether you lead a family, a team, a company, a community, or a nation—has a supreme responsibility to set expectations and then to help those they lead to meet those expectations.

It is the ultimate demonstration of love to help them meet those expectations by providing the resources, training, encouragement, and yes, even correction when they are failing to meet those expectations. How we provide the correction is what typically divides the great loving leader from the poor ineffective leader. The difference is not only in the tone of voice, but is usually in the correction's clarity, consistency, fairness, and timeliness.

The skill of reproving and holding followers accountable is an essential but commonly lacking skill that many emerging leaders will do well to master. Consider a leader who yells, who in anger embarrasses an individual in public, who sarcastically points out a failing or who even lets mistakes go on for long periods of time before finally "having had enough" and then makes an example of someone or some behavior. Compare that leader to a leader who sees a shortcoming, a mistake, or a pattern of weakness and quickly and privately helps the person or group of people to see how the work is unacceptable and then provides the instruction necessary as well as the resources that may be needed to better complete what is expected of them. I believe the majority of people actually want to do their best and in most cases where they come up short it's the leader's fault for not setting proper expectations.

Love Unfeigned in the Boardroom

Sometimes a demonstration of love and caring takes no words at all. I had just received a position serving as the number two guy to a president with responsibility over an organization with about 3,800 people. We were sitting in our first meeting with the department heads and their leadership teams.

The president had worked with these leaders for several years and knew them all. I knew very few of the 35 people packed into the small meeting room.

On a yellow pad, I wrote the names of the few leaders I knew, positioning their names on the page to reflect where they were sitting in the room. As each leader was called upon to speak, or was addressed by somebody else in the room, I discreetly added their name to my pad. My genius was working. Name after name was added to my page. Within a few minutes my self-assessment of genius quickly turned to admiration and appreciation for the president seated next to me. I almost chuckled as I recognized that early on he had noticed my effort and systematically directed the meeting in such a way as to call upon by name, each leader represented by a blank space on my yellow pad. Nothing was ever said. It wasn't until I completed my seating chart that the president called upon or took comments from any of the leaders I already knew. At that point I was invited to participate and was comfortably able to call upon leaders by name.

This was one of my first experiences in following this president so closely. I have since in word and deed learned that his pattern of leadership of "Know Them, Love Them, Serve Them," is very effective in exercising influence. Great leaders demonstrate that they love and care as they develop new leaders and work for the success of those they lead.

He demonstrated great leadership to me in several ways that night. It was evident that he wanted me to be more effective as I began this new role. He wanted the leaders in that room to feel that they were important and known to me as I interacted with them by name, and he has never mentioned it or taken credit for helping me out. In fact, he may not know I ever noticed his kindness. We have never spoken of it. Great leaders show great love as they work for the success of those they serve, especially when doing so without bringing attention to themselves.

I conclude with one last example.

Love Unfeigned in the Classroom

My father was killed in a plane crash the week I turned 16, leaving my mother to raise and provide for seven children. I had my eye on a college education, but I knew if there was any chance of getting there I would need a scholarship.

I was an art guy, not an academic who loved science, math or the other highly mentally demanding subjects. Despite being an art guy, I was on track for a scholarship, until an oil painting class with Clyde Smith – a tough, but highly respected art teacher. I took several classes from Mr. Smith and he and I got along well.

For our term assignment, which would carry most of our grade in the class, Mr. Smith assigned us to paint a portrait of someone live. Yes, that meant I had to get somebody to sit for dozens of hours while I painted their portrait. I finally got a girl I had dated to give me the time and pose for this assignment. Now, it's not a totally unpleasant assignment to sit for hours and look at a pretty girl. Though she didn't care for it so much, I put my heart into it – both figuratively as well as literally. Upon completion, it, along with all the other portraits from the class hung in the art lab. I was very proud of my painting; it was easily one of the best. You can imagine my heart break when it only garnered me a B.

The shock turned to despair, the despair to anger, and I went to see Mr. Smith and make my case. "How could this be only B work. I completed the assignment well, on time, with an actual model and it was clearly one of the best in the whole class?" Mr. Smith listened, nodded, agreed and simply said, "It may be the best in the class, but it's not your best."

If that B held, it could easily keep me from the college scholarship I so desperately wanted and needed.

I turned from logic and reason and pointed out what a B would do to my scholarship chances. Mr. Smith didn't budge. I got pathetic and started to beg. Nothing. I'm embarrassed to admit I then hit the bottom and began to make excuses why it couldn't be my best work – how if I only had better brushes, or better paints. As Mr. Smith listened, he picked up a stick from off his desk. I didn't even know why he had a stick on his desk. He pulled a knife from his pocket and carved a nice beveled point on the stick. Grabbing a piece of copy paper and a bottle of ink, he began a portrait of me. Stick and ink.

I stood there quietly and he drew. Nothing needed to be said. When he finished he handed it to me. I took it, thanked him for his nice art, and left.

The B stood firm and yes, eventually, it was enough to keep me from my academic scholarship. I was disgusted that I couldn't even get an A in what I did best.

Mr. Smith had made choices. He could have easily and justifiably given me the A that would have assured me the scholarship I wanted, and needed. I also believe he actually wanted me to get the scholarship. It was probably a hard choice, but he chose me and he wanted me to become a better me.

High school life went on. As a senior, we were all invited to enter the State-wide High School Art Competition held at the famed Springville Art Gallery. We could each enter 4 pieces – funny thing, of the 4 pieces I entered, the portrait of the girl I painted, wasn't good enough to be one of them.

After the judging, we eagerly made our way to Springville to see how we had all done. I was so impressed with the work from high school students from around the state. Our class did well – lots of ribbons, first places, Sweepstakes, Best in Show – all by my classmates. But not one ribbon on any of my pieces. Though happy for my friends, I left the show feeling pretty disappointed. The show lasted several more weeks.

One afternoon as we were just leaving home headed to the gallery to pick up my art, the phone rang and one of my buddies on the other end congratulated me. He had just returned from the gallery with his art. When I questioned him about the congratulations, he said I'd have to see for myself.

When we finally arrived, the gallery was mostly empty. Only a few remaining pieces hung on walls here and there. From across the gallery I could see my pieces abandoned, hanging all alone. As we crossed the empty room, I saw a small card tucked into the frame of my major piece and then I saw why congratulations were in order.

On the last day of the show, I had been awarded a full scholarship from Brigham Young University's very prestigious art program. Mr. Smith hadn't chosen to give me the A which would lead to a scholarship, he had chosen to give me a better me—a me qualified to earn that scholarship. Love Unfeigned.

As we all know, leadership is about influence. People will only "yield" to the influence of those they have learned to trust and respect. One of the surest ways to earn that trust and respect is through love unfeigned.

As shared here, there are many ways to demonstrate that love – personally, collectively, and organizationally. As leaders grow in their ability to influence others, their ability to love is often the defining characteristic that will set them apart as a true leader.

About the Author

While typical advertising creative types thrive on clever and cunning advertisements, they run in horror when asked if it worked. Not Kent, "ideas that work," are his passion. The ideas come easily, making them work takes discipline, and for his 35 years he and his creative teams have proven time and again their discipline works.

Coming directly out of college, Kent partnered with a dear friend and started an advertising agency in a small town in Northern Utah. Proving his ability to generate response, drive traffic, make the phone ring, and change perceptions with his creative, targeted messages, attracted clients such as Disney, VISA International, Discover Card, JCPenney, USPS, Comcast and many other local, regional and national companies.

Recognized on the international direct marketing stage as one of the leading creative trendsetters, Kent's "ideas that work" have won as many international Echo Awards as any single agency in the world. (Echo awards are given by the International Direct Marketing Association for creative advertising with proven success) Due to his success in creatively influencing consumers through his direct marketing, Kent has been a favored speaker at conferences and meetings in Asia, Eastern and Western Europe, Latin America and across the US. This experience has helped Kent develop the ability to create and present powerful and exciting content in such a way as to engage his audiences and drive the content deep into their understanding, thus ensuring its utilization by those who attend his programs.

This passion for creative and effective communications has naturally flowed into his approach to leadership in not only his business life, but in community service and at home. Not only has he run a successful advertising agency for 35 years, he has been leading large and small groups since he was a Boy Scout. He was chosen to lead the High School VICA clubs throughout the state of Utah while he was only a junior in high school. In his ecclesiastic responsibilities he has been able to preside over congregations both large and small.

Along with his wife of 37 years, they have employed the creative discipline "ideas that work" in raising their 5 children who are each successfully pursuing their chosen vocations and raising families of their own.

While still developing marketing and advertising "ideas that work" for wonderful local and national clients, Kent has increasingly been invited to apply his creative "ideas that work" to leadership development, helping veteran and emerging leaders to employ a proven discipline to their own leadership development. With that charge, and blending a life filled with leadership experience and a passion for creativity, Kent has now taken the General Theory of Leadership, along with its proven doctrines and principles of leadership and made leadership development fun, enjoyable, understandable, predictable and achievable.

A. Kent Merrell
Author, Speaker, Creative Director
801-652-3200
kent@mrdirect.com
kentmerrell.com

NATIONAL SPEAKERS ASSOCIATION

NSA®

MOUNTAIN WEST
Idaho, Montana, Utah, Wyoming

A Place of Love
Love is the Answer. Love is Also the Question.

by Becky Mackintosh

"At the end of the day people won't remember what you said or did, they will remember how you made them feel."

—Maya Angelou

How DO YOU make others feel? What if everything you did and said came from a place of love? *Then* would they remember what you did and said?

When we, intelligent human beings, deal with people in tough situations such as family fights, professional disagreements, organizational conflict, or political controversy, we have a tendency to line up the facts in our minds like little tin soldiers. We make sure that we are right. We check our facts and information and to secure we are coming from the right place.

That's pretty good. We should come from the right place. But what is the right place?

Perhaps the bigger question is, are we coming from a place of love?

As I have traveled the world, people are the same. No matter your profession, demographics, location, social status, educational degree or religious beliefs; no matter whether you are rich, poor, brown, black, white, pink or green – we all have the same basic needs.

We all want to feel loved, safe, appreciated, trusted, respected, accepted and valued for whom we are and the diversity we bring. Right?

It has been my experience that treating people the way you want to be treated keeps customers coming back, employees giving a 100%, and a puts a smile not only on your face, but on others' too.

Have you ever stopped to think that regardless of what type family you come from—whether it is a traditional nuclear family, a stepfamily, a single-parent family, an adopted family, or a single-person-with-a-pet family—it consists of those who care about each other?

And that's what it really boils down to – caring about one another and feeling you belong and are valued. And loved!

If you are irritated with someone – or just don't like them much – everything they do or say is going to bother you. But when you really care about a person they could spill an entire plate of food onto your lap and you'd probably laugh – and make sure *they* were okay. It's true. Why is that?

When something like that happens will you act kindly or react harshly? It's a choice. Wayne Dyer is right: "Change the way you look at things and the things you look at change." You see situations, circumstances, and people in a different perspective.

Coming from a place of being right, is reasonable. Coming from a place of love has nothing to do with reason or being right – but it works. Try it. Feel it. You'll see how it really is more "right" than being right!

Of course, no one is perfect at everything; but you can be perfect at some things. You can be perfect at trying to be perfectly kind, perfectly loving, and always coming from a place of love.

To create a positive environment, in the workplace or at home, look for the good in every situation. Positive reinforcement goes much further than criticism. When you learn a better way, when you commit to do better, confidence grows. Confidence and commitments grow exponentially when a person feels valued and especially when they feel loved.

And your personal payback is wonderful. You feel better, you even look better! Did you know that a simple act of kindness benefits your health by boosting the immune system and reducing your heart rate? A *simple act of kindness* actually triggers the brain's pleasure center, releasing endorphins - *the feel good happy chemical*. It also reduces wrinkles. Can't beat that! An act of kindness costs you nothing and saves you much.

Advanced imaging technology reports that the human brain is wired to reward caring, cooperation, and service.

Merely thinking about someone experiencing harm triggers the same reaction in our brain as when a mother sees distress in her baby's face. Conversely, According to the research documented by David Korten in *Yes! Magazine, Nov 2008, We are hard-wired to care and connect.* Korten says, "The act of *helping* [emphasis added] another triggers the brain's pleasure center and benefits our health by boosting our immune system, reducing our heart rate, and preparing us to approach and soothe. Positive emotions like compassion produce similar benefits." Negative emotions suppress our immune system, increase heart rate, and prepare us for fight or flight.

Your mother said it, your grandmother too. *"'Do unto others as you would have them do unto you.' That's the golden rule!"*

But what happens when the golden rule is challenged – *really* challenged? How do you respond then? Does the rule become obsolete because you are certain it was not intended for you in this situation?

It is easy to be positive and optimistic when all things are going well, but what happens when things aren't going so well?

What if your faith and world as you know it is shaken due to unforeseen circumstances?

What happens when what you hoped and dreamed for all of your life and envisioned as your plan for yourself and for your family is thrown off course? Someone in your family gets divorced. No one planned for that, right? So are you now a failed family? No, you are just a family with a different situation and perhaps more complex relationships.

Do you turn into a dysfunctional family because your unwed daughter gets pregnant? What if your child is enslaved to drugs, alcohol, pornography or some other addiction? Are you now a failed family? No, you just become a family with a particular set of circumstances that needs special attention.

What if you find out your child is gay? Are you now a failed family? No. You are a family with a member who needs special love and understanding and who has love and understanding to give back.

If these scenarios are indications of failure – then I have a failed family.

But, wait; remember what Maya Angelou said. *"At the end of the day people won't remember what you said or did, they will remember how you made them feel."*

My husband Scott and I have not failed because of our focus on staying in the right place – a place of love.

I know what it is like to be the mother to an unwed pregnant daughter. I know what it feels like to be a mother to a gay son. And as difficult as those things were when they presented themselves, approaching them from a place of love created beauty and wonder instead of disaster. I wouldn't trade my set of circumstances for anything in the world. These things were not on my vision board. I could not have prepared myself for these events, except to focus on the positive and try always to approach difficult situations – every situation – from a place of love.

As you take a look around at the amount of judgment and hatred in the world, couldn't the honest response be that we all could do better? We, the human race, are here to love one another, serve one another and do our very best to help one another with the challenges and trials that come our way.

Jesus' counsel in John 13:34 to "Love one another as I have loved you," means what it says. Love *everyone* – even those among our families and friends that may make different choices than we would. Intolerance creates hate, war, bullying, sadness and pain. That needs to stop. Love needs to start.

Gandhi said: "Be the change you wish to see in the world."

This was personally put to a test when my belief system was challenged and my world turned upside down.

It was January 9, 2012, when my 24-year-old son, Sean, told his father Scott and I that he was gay. Sean is a millennial, so he told us the best way he knew how – in a Facebook private message.

Precisely at 11:11 pm, he sent us this:

> *"Hey so I'm not gonna beat around the bush too much, I'm just going to tell you something that I'm sure you already know or it has at least crossed your mind plenty of times. I'm gay. I'm sure this isn't the best news a parent could hear, but I feel like it's not right for me to not talk to you about something very real to me. I want you to know I'm very much the same weird Sean. Ha! I love you and Dad so much and you're the best parents a kid could ask for. This is why it's taken me so long to tell you, I'm fine with the pain it can bring me at times; but I just didn't want to hurt you 'cause you don't deserve it. Once again I love you very much, but I want to keep this brief because I am sure you'd rather talk in person and I am one hundred percent fine with that. I haven't told anyone ever, I wanted you and Dad to be the first to know."*

The sting of reading the words "I'm gay" was soothed by his last sentence:

> *"I haven't told anyone, ever. I wanted you and Dad to be the first to know."*

That validated how awesome, amazing, and considerate my son is. It let me know that we could deal with this if we approached it from the only place possible – a place of love. We loved our son. He loved us. Therefore, somehow, it would all work out.

What concerned me, was the fact that my son had hidden deep in a closet, and had secured with lock and key, his most conflicted and torn feelings – and had dealt with them all alone, by himself, for years.

That, I was not proud of.

Sean was correct in his assumption that this had "at least crossed my mind." I had often wondered about my strikingly good-looking son that only dated when girls took the initiative and asked him out. It was something I kept quiet and secret, hardly daring to think even to myself. I hoped it was not true, but

I had wondered. And there it was in black and white on my computer view screen – my son's courageous announcement that he was gay.

His father had no clue. Scott was blindsided by the news. It shook him to his core. Those words "I'm gay" coming from his son were not on Scott's Family Vision Board either. Scott had no clue as to how to acknowledge his son and reply to this heartfelt, vulnerable message. Except he knew he loved his son; and that, as it turned out, was enough.

Immediately upon reading Sean's message, I responded by asking him to hurry home so we could talk, face-to-face. This was Sean's final night before heading back to school in Hawaii. He was out visiting friends and saying his goodbyes for a new year. When he got home, we stayed up until four in the morning talking, crying, and hugging before calling it a night and heading to the airport a few hours later. Oh, how difficult that last hug was for Scott and me; but it would have to suffice for an entire year.

➤•◄

I am not proud of everything I said in that very first conversation. I said some things completely out of ignorance. I had never researched the subject, naively thinking that it was something other families had to deal with – not mine.

First, I told Sean I loved him and that my love would *never* change. I felt very strongly that he needed to know of my unconditional love for him. That was good. Then I said some really ignorant stuff like: "What are you going to do about it?" and "You are a fighter Sean – you can fight this." "Hang in there. This is your test – your challenge."

As these phrases spilled off my lips, I honestly thought I was giving words of comfort. I didn't know each phrase was a dagger in my son's heart. Why? Because I was busy "fixing" the "problem" in my son rather than simply hearing him from a place of love.

The words weren't new to my son. He had grown up hearing them everywhere – and he had spent a lifetime trying to digest and understand why he felt the way he felt and what kind of life that meant for him.

What broke my heart that evening was looking at my 24-year-old son, and thinking my adorable little boy with the big smile had grown up dealing with this secret all alone. He had no one to trust and talk to about this, one of the most important things in his life, likely the most difficult and challenging. I cried then, and I cry still now at the thought of thousands of Lesbian Gay Bisexual Transgender (LGBT) youth dealing with their situations and fears and feelings of inadequacy – and doing it alone, afraid to talk about their true feelings and contemplating suicide as the answer.

Death is not the answer. Love is the answer. Love is also the question.

I listened to my son tell us what it was like growing up "fighting that inward battle" and trying to "fit in" into a world that frowns upon gays. My heart broke at the thought of *my own flesh and blood* feeling like a misfit right in my home, in schools, in society, and within the walls of the church that we love. I realized that the pain and loneliness would have completely dissolved if everyone would simply look at these children of God with love – from a place of love.

While growing up, Sean never revealed the sadness or the confusion going on inside. He wore the mask very well since we saw him as a very happy, active, fun-loving boy and teenager. We didn't know. His friends didn't know. But Sean knew. He acted as if he was just like everyone else – never revealing his inner turmoil and conflicts. If an Oscar could be awarded, he would have won.

My heart felt pierced with daggers when I replayed Sean's words telling me of how many times during his tender years he contemplated ending his life so no one would ever find out he was gay. I am saddened that he, and so many millions like him, ever felt that level of despair. I am so thankful Sean never acted upon those dark feelings. Today he is happy with who he is and with the person he is becoming. It is my prayer and personal quest that we create a world where everyone feels accepted and loved.

I have researched, Googled, blogged, fasted and prayed to become more educated. One startling fact that I learned in my quest to gain knowledge and understanding is that teens and young adults who identify as gay, lesbian, bi-sexual, transgender or same-sex attraction have one of the highest rates of suicide attempts over all other groups studied. That is unacceptable! No one should go to bed at night thinking they are better off dead. No one. We need to be the change we so desire to see in the world. We need to love one another; serve one another; help one another.

This isn't just about being gay. It's about being different. It's about every person on the planet wanting to fit in – to feel loved, safe, respected, accepted and valued for who they are. It's about responding to people and situations from a place of love, compassion, and willingness to walk in another's shoes.

Life's not fair. In fact, it's a roller coaster ride with twist and turns and loop-de-loops. When we love people unconditionally, we create a positive, profound ripple effect that gets them safely through the ride. Hearts are healed, families are reunited, and lives are saved.

What if everything you did and said came from a place of love? We all could do a bit better in this arena, don't you think? I know I could.

No matter your profession, demographics, location, social status, education, or your religious beliefs; no matter whether you are rich, poor, brown, black, white, pink or green – we all have the same basic need and that is to love and be loved.

Love. Love unconditionally. It. Is. A. Choice. It is *the* choice.

About the Author

Challenged by your children? Traumatized by your teens? Relationships on the rocks?

Love is the answer.

Love is also the question.

Becky Mackintosh; mother, grandmother, speaker, author, humanitarian and positivity-clarity coach, believes that coming from a place of love is the single most effective and influential parenting and relationship tool we have.

With strength gained from her own difficult past, Becky Mackintosh applies her life lessons raising seven children, and a husband. Experience and love equip Becky with the what it takes to motivate people, persuade organizations and elevate families to developing self esteem, self confidence, and fortifying relationships.

Becky Mackintosh is the author of "My Husband Wears The Short Shorts In THIS Family! Parenting with Humor, Courage and a Whole Lot of Love."

She and her husband Scott have been featured on: Good Morning America, TODAY, Rachael Ray, CNN, Inside Edition, The Browser 5.0, The Matt Townsend Show, Behind the Mask Radio, Fox 13 – and the list goes on.

Becky Mackintosh
Life's Short Lessons LLC
Lehi, Utah
(801) 372-6277
bmackintosh22@msn.com
BeckyMacksBlog.com
https://www.facebook.com/becky.courtmackintosh
@BeckyMack22
@BeckyMack22
LifesShortLessons.com

NATIONAL SPEAKERS ASSOCIATION

NSA

MOUNTAIN WEST
Idaho, Montana, Utah, Wyoming

Elevate Your Efforts to Greatness!

by Brandon Kelly

WAYNE HAMMETT WAS a towering, yet slender figure that loved to volunteer as a coach for at-risk youth and help them discover that there was something more to an individual than what they could see in themselves. His forte was working with these inner city youths to build their confidence and help them set records in their own rights. He knew that even though they were kids and they were lacking confidence, sooner or later they would grow up and need to gain confidence through real-life experiences as well as desire to win, if they but only experienced how. So he set out to inspire and challenge youth to find their greatness.

Such was my case in 1988 when I met him.

I found myself radically smaller than the rest of the students. I got beat up daily in the fifth grade and choose to join a real life gang for the protection—at least so that if someone did pick on me I could have the backup and support of a larger group, I reasoned. After school we hung out on the school playgrounds playing pick-up games of football or basketball while we watched the school teams practice for their competitions across the field. The coach kept a watchful eye on us, but he was actually concerned for our wellbeing. We found out he was concerned that if we got too deep into the gang there might not be any going back or helping us out of it.

He could tell that Shermaine and I were different from the rest of the 4-Horseman gang. Neither of us were involved with the bad activities they were doing and we would play great as team. He was tall and I was small. He was athletically gifted, and I was scrappy—walking with a limp from a near-fatal accident with a drunk driver when I was almost two years old. Together we excelled and helped each other out by reading the other's moves like we were brothers.

Coach Hammett finally invited the two of us to try out for both his basketball and track teams. After the tryouts he informed Shermaine he won a spot on both teams. As for me, I needed to be taller, faster, and more "coordinated." However, there was a caveat for me, that if I would work hard over the summer, I could try out for the teams again and perhaps fill a slot in the last spot on the team. He required us to get out of the gang before we could represent our school. We thought it was love or pride for the school so we agreed, doing what we could to get ourselves out not knowing how it would change our lives and define how we measured success.

From Gang into the Game

Little did we know that he loved to see people succeed while overcoming obstacles in their life, and that is why we were chosen. Our acceptance of that challenge saved our lives in ways that we could never imagine. The next few months were tough, but fruitful. Shermaine would teach me the techniques he was learning and in turn I would practice them until I couldn't walk anymore for the day. Together we helped each other improve to higher levels while our former gang members that made choices to hurt other people or cause long term trouble for themselves.

Coach Hammett saw me struggling with walking and running from a residual effect of the accident. He realized I had a hidden super power, if trained properly, or redirected the use of that disability to become my best asset. The secret was spring like power in my legs. One leg was shorter and the muscles were tighter than the other, which created a hidden spring effect that I could use to jump higher than all of the other players. We spent a lot of time at practice strengthening my weakness into resources.

He said, "All you need is a good kick, like I had inside of me, to accomplish great things!"

We were blessed to have a volunteer coach who had great passion about our being our best and becoming great men. He had a knack for creating practice systems that broke down barriers while replacing them with structure, teamwork, as well as a can-do attitude. I had found my way out. More importantly, I found someone who believed in me and gave me a chance to become something great, instead of the shortfalls that others saw at the time.

Time to Take a Stand

I had been asked to compete in the high jump and three other distance track events for our school. It was a hurdle that grows and grows, how could it be conquered? At first I was scared and kept knocking down the high bar at the starting height of three feet due to the old twin mattress with springs sticking out for our landing pad. I would run up to the bar and try to hop over it like a hurdle instead of leveling my body out with all of my energy to get above the bar. Even after several attempts and practices I could still not manage to clear the bar.

Coach Hammett saw the tiny acorn of strength and potential to do good for others in me when I did not see it in myself.

He would sit the high jumpers on the bench and point his long pencilly fingers in our faces, urgently trying to help what our job was. "The bar is our friend and not our enemy! We have to see above the bar and see how to overcome it, and only then can we see ourselves winning! We have to elevate our efforts to get over the bar! We are winners! Now get back out there and show me how it's done," Coach would exclaim.

WOW!!! Those truths still resonate with me to this day and apply to every hurdle and obstacle that we may face in life! The bar simply measures where we are and how much room we have to grow and improve!

I whispered to Coach that he had the wrong kid for this event. I was not the right build and I was too small compared to the others. How could I possibly run and jump like the other kids because of my limp? I was convinced that I was not a runner nor a high jumper and all of these fears seemed so real to me. Then Coach pulled me aside and asked me if I knew the story of Wilma Rudolph. I had no clue who she was.

Wilma was born premature, fairly sick most of her life, and wished to see herself playing with the other kids, running and jumping without the metal brace that wrapped around her thin legs. All of which kept her from finding joy. She decided to become a runner and diligently worked to get her body in shape. She then competed in the 1960 Olympic Games in Rome, Italy, as a 20-year-old woman. Others told her she was too young or too small, yet she became the first female American runner to win Gold. She also went on to win two other events during that Olympics and came home with three gold medals and a coveted World Record. Doctors told her she would never walk, but her mother told her she would run—she just had to imagine it in her head. She believed her mother and she won!" Coach proclaimed.

"Do you believe me when I say you were made to jump and run and win? You are the right height and build to get over the bar. Let me teach you and you can show the world!"

I had no reason not to believe my coach, so I dutifully followed his training and practice regimen. He taught me to approach the hurdles and the high bars by measuring it off, standing next to them, then letting them know that I was not afraid of them anymore. I was going to get over them so they should not stand in my way. We were a team working together to win, and, finally, that I would clear the bar and stand on the mat in victory with my arms waving above my head because I kicked my gimpy leg out of the way and over the bar to a new level of personal success.

Time to Raise the Bar by Elevating Your Efforts

The big day came for Shermaine and I to compete at the statewide sixth grade track meet in the high jump and distance events. I surveyed the other competitors who were 5'-8" to 6'-0" tall, all in the sixth grade and much more capable of clearing these high marks than my little frame of 5'-3". I again wondered if I was big enough to compete with the others and if I could do my school justice in the competition. *Did my coach choose the right person? Could I even do it*, I fretted.

Everything seemed bigger than real life at that high school, and we anxiously awaited our event to be announced. Time ticked on ever so slowly. Then, without warning, they announced over the loudspeaker that for the next thirty minutes that the high jump event would be held on the south end of the field by the football goal posts, and the competitors needed to check in.

Butterflies swarmed my stomach along with a huge case of stage fright. This was only the first of my events! I got up and meandered to the high jump area where I gazed at the growing hurdle called the high jump; now filled with the largest amount of doubt and even fear that I would not be able to do it. *Was I going to be the one that let my coach and school down? Should I even check in?*

I contemplated how I was going to jump over the bar when it already seemed twice as high as it was when we practiced back in the gym with the thin mattresses. I stood there on my own little island not knowing what to do or where to begin when I unexpectedly remembered what it took to A.C.E. the situation--the formula for raising performance that I had learned. I needed to stand up and face my challenge, count off my paces, race to mark my jumping spot so that I would not miss the prime landing area, and then trace back my steps like Coach Hammett had drilled us on. *I could do this!* I reasoned.

Others painfully crashed into the bar making it look agonizing. I wanted to make sure that I was way above the bar so that I did not have to experience the pain of failing or not making it to the next height. Soon enough it was my turn and I took off faster than normal, hoping I would clear the bar and not crash into it or have to use all of my turns and be eliminated as other boys already had done. I found myself soaring above the bar by nearly two feet on my first attempt. I was already in the five-foot level. Surely that would be in winning contention, and all I had to do was jump like that again!

Shermaine on the other hand, would crash into the bar on his first attempt. He leapt too late, wrapping his legs around the pole and wracking himself on the second attempt as he dismantled the high jump equipment sending it everywhere. He was not only visibly hurting but looked exhausted from the failed attempts. Hunched over griping his shorts, panting, and trying to recover from the recent injury before the third and final try he would he said, "I can't go any farther or run another step it hurts too much."

I was inspired to share with him that all he needed to do was, "Jump a little higher and see above the bar." He did just that, and together we raised the bar to new heights like we had done on the court. After two hours of raising the bar a quarter of an inch at a time, we moved past the five- and nearly to the six-foot mark until we had eliminated all of the competition and only we remained.

Now it was just two friends from the same school, and even once from the same gang, competing to see who would win. On Shermaine's third and final attempt at the 6'-3" mark, he epically crashed into the bar just one inch before the state record for our age group. He dragged the bar and the whole high jump system to the ground underneath him for the last time.

I was done and had won, right? After all, I was the last man standing. Coach came to me and said, "Are you going to seize the moment and go for the gold record like Wilma Rudolph or just go home with first place?" (These words have been the hallmarks that I have used to measure everyday achievements since then!)

He was right, I had only one more inch to go to break the record. But my strength had waned to the point that I wasn't sure if I had it in me to take one more fatigued step. *Was I a quitter or a winner?* I shouted to the coach and the staff to raise the bar to 6'-5", two full inches from where it presently was, but at a new record level. I stared at the obstacle for what seemed like hours until the final warning whistle blew seconds later. I was searching the depths of my soul to see if there was anything left in me. Admittedly, *I was out of gas.* I was done and I knew it, but I had just thrown down the gauntlet. I wanted to prove to everyone that I could do it and that I was just as good as they were. Words kept echoing in my head, "Was it going to be just first place or first place with a new state record?" *Would I fulfill that dream of winning the event? Where would I get the energy? What was I going to do? If it was to be, it was certainly up to me!*

Measuring up to my full 5'-3" gangly self I suddenly—even with without thinking—started sprinting faster than I had run before, straight at the tallest obstacle I had faced so far in both the competition and life. I rehearsed how many paces it was, and knew that I had to kick higher than ever before, strapping on hidden wings to fly over the bar at this height. I sailed past the record mark and into state history! As my team and coach embraced me, I realized that I could overcome anything and knew that I still had a few more jumps remaining in my fatigued legs.

By the end of the day I had set the new record at 6'-7 ½" and took four other records home in speed and distance running for my team, all from the energy of winning and triumphing over self-imposed limitations. The high jump record still stands to this printing.

The doctors from my car accident and the majority of people around me said I would never participate in events like this and should not even try. Instead I suddenly believed I could win and I went home with several first places and a record just like Wilma because I listened to my coach and visualized the win versus doubting unseen abilities.

My heart was beating like a bass drum—the heartbeat of my new life of being successful and overcoming fears. Others had told me not to participate, but now I was a winner. Believing in my dreams and burying their comments was the key to overcoming challenges and never letting my disability hold me back again!

Learning to Love Yourself to Elevate Your Efforts

There are several lessons that can be learned from Coach Hammett and the events of the high jump. We can triumph over our personal roadblocks if we put our mind to it. You do not have to participate in competitive events to prove that you are a winner. No matter where you have come from in life you can overcome your hurdles while setting new high bench marks in all you do with a can-do approach.

Next, don't hide from the good inside. Everyone has good on the inside that, if cultivated and believed in, will turn the average person into great one in their own realm. Once you find what you are good at or need to improve at, you need to keep pursuing it until you are renowned for it. Now you are on the stage called "Life" and the outcome depends on you. The immortal Shakespeare once said that "all the world is a stage," but we need to realize that we are the main character and the performance that is delivered will be up to us and how we have practiced and trained for the winning round. Make every moment your masterpiece moment and you will win the accolades that you deserve.

You need to face your hurdles and stand tall next to them. As you do they will become seemingly smaller and have less of an effect on you until they no longer impede your path. As you stand tall you gain the confidence that was needed but that you felt might be latent in your character. The hurdles and the high bars become a measuring point of what you are capable of rising above— no longer a picture of what is holding you back—but of what you have become!

You get to set the pace to get over the bar. Fast or slow, some hurdles and high bars need an immediate reaction to beat the deadline. Others can be prepared for and anticipated as you balance out the effort that it will take to set your mark. Make sure you plan time to know which steps are critical and how long it will take to conquer the obstacle to win while avoiding the distractions.

Dig in until you win! When you feel it is time to quit, that is the precise time to dig in deeper while you continue the quest to give every last ounce and breath to triumph over that hurdle. Continue past the fear and drive with determination to the finish line. This will stretch your ability as it builds your capacity. The triumph will give you the energy that is needed to continue on to the next quest.

You can raise the high mark higher simply by setting your sights higher than you have ever done before. Do not settle. Do not let mediocrity set in. Do not settle for first place. Instead focus on setting the record while you leave your distinctive high mark. Would we have landed on the moon if we stopped with jet propulsion? Only then can you see what you are made of and where you will leave your mark.

Because of that belief that we all have to help others out and up, the more people that you help in the process of achieving your dreams, the better you will become as you find yourself surrounded by greatness simply by being willing to improve.

We should look at others like Coach Wayne Hammett, seeing the value in a fallen acorn with a hard shell that had the potential to become a mighty oak tree if cultivated properly. Like Coach Hammett, we should be looking for the best in the situation while we look to the future of what will come from helping others achieve their greatness instead of the hard shell they are in presently. It is not what others see for you in life that matters, but what you see for yourself as you prepare for that moment of triumph that really counts. Once you decide that there is greatness in you and that you are capable of achieving your greatness, nothing can stand in your way as long as you're committed to the outcome.

You need to believe that you are worthy of success. You're capable of achieving and leaving your own Watermark of Distinction. Perhaps you have not tried or have not been successful in other areas of your life, but now is the time to prove yourself. There is so much potential and room for each one of us to shine and perfect the things that we are good at. We just need to jump into the game of life so we can leave everything that we've got on the field.

Every one of us gets kicked down, pulled back, or has an insurmountable obstacle placed in front of us throughout life. It is all in how we face our obstacles that determines whether we win. Each of us can raise the bar from a mere obstacle to be a world-class competitor in everything that we do daily if we will focus on the "can" versus the "cannot" of the situation.

I knew that no matter the pain, or the challenge that must be overcome, if there was anything out there that people said I could not do, I would go and do it to prove them wrong. You too can overcome your hurdles as you believe in yourself and decide to stand up and stand out instead of float under the radar.

We can learn from Coach Hammett that we need to dig in until we win and love to help others rise above their challenges like a good mentor teaches. This way we learn to love to elevate our efforts as we face the ups and downs in lives.

Finally, Always Champion Excellence to be the Ace that sets your own records in everything you do in life. What more needs to be said than focusing on the two first places that matter most: winning against yourself and doing your best. The ace becomes the primary person that is relied on and counted on to bring home the win no matter the odds, you can overcome the challenge to win if you will Dig in to Win and Elevate Your Efforts so you can Elevate Your Excellence!

Take the advice of Coach Hammett and face your hurdles and stand a little bit taller in everything you do. You are a gold medalist, now perform like one!

About the Author

Brandon B. Kelly is a international speaker, trainer, and business improvement expert. He is the author of *The Distinctive Watermark Principles: How to Elevate Your Efforts to Greatness and Stand out in ALL You Do*, and *ABC's of Business Survival, Thrival, and Revival in the modern economy.*

Brandon sets records everywhere he goes including setting a high jump record that has stood since 1989 and prepared him to try out for the Olympics later in life. He has successfully coached and mentored dozens of businesses in multiple industries using the techniques of raising the bar, as well as fighting cancer twice, survived two critical dump truck accidents all while accomplishing over 2,500 of his goals—after being told he only had months to live in 1993 as a 16 year old over a span of 6 years.

Brandon has directed the startup of six businesses after he served as VP of Sales and also as CEO in several companies and is known for his out-of-the-box approach to finding a winning solution to business challenges. He has extensive experience in many facets of leadership, management and business.

Brandon has had leadership and adventure in all 50 states and over 30+ countries. He was presented Baden-Powell Fellow Award, the second highest award for serving youth in Scouting around the world by the HMS King of Sweden while a guest of HMS Queen of England in 2007.

Enjoy his formulas for success while we Elevate our Efforts to Elevate Your Excellence!

Brandon Kelly, PhD
President of Eagle Consulting
Brandon@TheBrandonKelly.com
TheBrandonKelly.com
ElevateYourEffort.com

To Live Your Dream,
You Have to Do it Your Own Way

by Chad Hymas

THIS IS NOT real. This can't be real.

I am a head, locked in a brace, bolted to the wall. My head is held motionless and nothing else has the power to move. I have no body – no arms, no legs – at least, nothing I can sense.

My head is all that I am and all that I have; and it is held captive in a device of torture – that non-angelic halo brace. I can't move a single part of what once was me.

What isn't paralyzed and numb radiates incessant pain. I didn't know there were so many kinds of pain – dull aches from not moving; sharp unrelenting pain from those four pointed screws piercing my skull, dull thumping headache pain; throbbing pain from where I attempted to chew a hole in my lip to breathe; and deep, permeating nausea from shock and medication.

Boredom, futility, and hopelessness engulf me as I lie staring at the stark white composite ceiling. I can no longer hope to accomplish the dreams that lent enthusiasm and energy to my life. Life is over as I know it. I am convinced.

A little over a century ago, Nietzsche, a well-known German philosopher and philologist, said, "Convictions are more dangerous enemies of truth than lies."

He believed in the honest questioning of any belief that drains one of enthusiasm for life. Nietzsche is right. We should have the courage of our convictions; but also the courage to question our convictions, especially when those convictions lead us to dismay or despair. As I think of all that I have lost, I certainly am in dismay and despair.

These thoughts darken my mood, but in comes the cavalry to the rescue. I could almost hear bugles and pounding hooves.

It's Dad.

Dad has become my own personal, self-appointed motivational speaker. He begins with gentle enthusiasm, "Son, I know this seems impossible, but…"

I know he's trying to be helpful. I know he is coming from a place of love and he doesn't want me to give up on life. But what does he know? Was he ever paralyzed from his neck to his toes? What qualifies him to understand what I am going through?

Dad may not have been paralyzed, but something did happen that helps him understand. Three months before my accident, Dad and his wife Terrie were attending a national business convention in Dallas, Texas. The keynote speaker was introduced: Hall of Fame speaker, Art Berg, a C6-quadriplegic from Salt Lake City, Utah.

Dad sat spellbound as this amazing presenter talked about overcoming life's difficulties:

> *"Dreams are never destroyed by circumstance. They live or die in your heart. My dreams come true not in spite of my circumstance but because of it... For those of us in this life who are afraid to change, life will change for us. Then it is always a more painful experience... Dream new dreams or dream old dreams in new ways. Think new thoughts or think old thoughts in new ways... The miracles of our lives do not come about by grand events, but by the little things we have chosen to do... The biggest problems come about, because I avoid the little things too long... The difficult takes time; the impossible just takes a little longer."*

Never in his life had Dad been as moved as he was by Art's presentation. As soon as he returned home, he contacted his three sons and told us he had a wonderful video of an amazing presentation and we all needed to get together and watch it.

We never did.

Now, here I am, three months later, a quadriplegic, just like Art Berg. And here is my dad coming to the rescue.

"Son, what if I told you that you could be happier, more productive, and more successful with no hands and no legs than you ever were with them?"

I give him a look of utter disbelief, manage to force a mumbled "grrrmph" past the breathing tube and close my eyes stubbornly.

For a long moment, my dad looks at me with a mixture of understanding and disappointment. Then, without another word, he simply turns and walks away. He doesn't see a hurt kid. He sees an adult who isn't willing to be taught or to challenge his own despairing beliefs and conviction that all is lost.

I "grrrmph" again only in a different tone, desperately, with open and pleading eyes. This time "grrrmph" means, "Wait, don't leave. Dad, please don't leave." I begin to cry. I am a 27-year-old adult, married and a father of two children; but right now, I am the child and I need my dad. Like a child cries in the middle of the night, I cry for Dad to not leave me alone with this nightmare. I'll listen to his motivational speech if I have to. I really need him with me.

He pauses at the door. Turns. Dead serious. "Will you listen to what I have to say? Will you really listen to me, Son?"

Dad has just asked me if I could believe that I could be happier in a broken body than I ever was when I was whole. I am not buying it, but I don't want him to leave. After all, what else could he say that could be more unbelievable than saying I can be happier and more successful in this wreck of a body? That is just plain stupid. But I don't want to be alone, so I manage to push a halfhearted, "sure" past the breathing tube.

Dad comes back. He slides a videotape into the hospital room VCR. It is Art Berg's signature speech, "The Impossible Just Takes a Little Longer."

"Son, watch this."

I watch the tape without protest. What else am I going to do? I can't even turn my head.

When the speech is over, I don't remember one thing Art said. I do now; because I've watched it since – many times – and I still watch it every so often to remind myself of how possible impossible is. But I didn't really hear it then.

What I did notice was Art's body movement. How he contorted his body in order to move. Kind of a stretching, twisting movement he did occasionally as he spoke. I didn't understand it then. I understand it now.

I also notice his hands – when he gestures. His hands look like – well, they look like mine do now. Our hands are the same. Our bodies are the same. There is one thing we did not share, however. Art Berg is smiling. I am not. He laughs. I can't. The guy is happy. I'm miserable. I sure do notice that!

A few weeks later, my hospital room door suddenly bumps open and in rolls Art Berg. He is in a manual – not electric – wheelchair. I recognize him from the video. He looks like me. His hands are clenched, his fingers curled into his palms. He has minimal movement in his torso. His legs don't move at all.

He doesn't say his name. He doesn't say, "Hi, Chad." He doesn't say anything. He just wheels over to my bed, picks himself up out of his chair, and throws himself onto my bed.

Can you believe that? He lifts himself up out of his wheelchair and flops over onto my bed – without help! I had no idea that anyone in my circumstance could transfer, unaided, from chair to bed or from anywhere to anywhere, for that matter. How does he do that?

This guy's a quadriplegic. He has no stomach muscles, no chest muscles – none that work. No usable hands or forearms. He just pushes himself up. How?

I manage a surprised, "Hello?"

He doesn't reply, except to grin. Then he starts taking off his clothes.

He has my attention.

Art takes off his shirt without the use of his fingers. He undoes his belt with a little invention he made with wire. He removes his jeans. *Then he puts it all back on* – essentially with no workable hands or fingers – and arms that are 90% paralyzed.

Now he really has my attention.

After his little strip tease show, Art transfers back to his wheelchair, fishes around in a bag and pulls out a copy of his book, "Some Miracles Just Take a Little Longer." He signs it and hands it to me. He just did that with paralyzed hands and fingers. How?

What a demonstration! He isn't getting paid for this life-altering performance. He does it out of the goodness of his heart. He is teaching me. He is inspiring me. He is giving me confidence and hope – off the speaker's platform. He is challenging me to challenge my own beliefs – particularly my conviction that my life is over.

Maybe that's what great speakers and authors do best; inspire others to challenge their limiting beliefs; give them confidence and hope; and do it all the time, not just while on stage or in the pages of our books. Every waking, breathing moment we should live our message. It is important to walk our talk, so to speak, and whenever we speak, speak encouragement and hope. It helps *us,* too. What we do off the platform gives us greater presence and authenticity than while we're on it.

At this time, however, I don't really make the connection that Art is a speaker. I just see a happy, paralyzed guy giving an unhappy paralyzed guy the greatest gift of all – hope. Not by preaching, but simply by *doing.* Doing what? Doing simple things that are no longer simple for me – things I consider outside my range of possibility.

For the next nine months, I stay in close contact with him. I learn from him, am inspired and encouraged by him. I am always bugging someone to help me email him with all kinds of questions. He answers every email.

We have interesting parallels. Like me, Art is the father of two children, and husband to a beautiful woman. Like me, he became paralyzed just when his life was going really great. Like me, he is struck down in his prime. But rather than stay down, which no one would have blamed him for, he moves forward.

Art has a wonderful career traveling the world, speaking to civic groups, schools and churches, small businesses, professional associations, hospitals, and medical and huge corporate conventions.

Could I be like him? Can I move like him? Can I move *forward* like him? Can I be a good husband and father? Can I have a rewarding career? Can I have any kind of career? Everyone needs someone to look up to, someone to guide them—especially through difficult times when our business or personal life takes an unexpected turn.

Mine has sure taken a turn – upside-down!

Art helps me turn it right side up again.

Family, friends, therapists and doctors do wonders for me. However, Art does something no one else can do. He lets me look deep into his personal world – his quadriplegic world. This man is president-elect of the National Speakers Association, an NSA Hall of Fame speaking professional with a thriving business that keeps him traveling thousands of miles a year, speaking to audiences all around the globe. Yet here he is, focusing time and attention on me; someone he didn't even know until the day he rolled into my hospital room.

He brings me into his home and into his life. He lets me watch him operate his business, do housework like a real man, and, most importantly, he lets me watch as he takes care of his personal needs like shaving, dressing, brushing his teeth, etc.

Sharing the "etc" – the really personal stuff – is incredibly helpful and encouraging. I begin to understand on a very real level that I can be "normal," as long as I have the strength to challenge my convictions, and am willing to be "normal" differently.

Art isn't just a business and family man. He is an athlete. Truly. He plays full contact wheelchair rugby. These gutsy athletes don't let their disabilities stop them from competing. They throw themselves around with reckless abandon in wheelchairs that closely resemble demolition-derby cars. The Denver Harlequins, a quadriplegic rugby team, has an interesting motto: "It ain't real, if it don't bend steel!"

Competition? Hmmm... can I do that?

How about Art's 1993 marathon? Ten years after an auto accident costs him the use of his legs and severely limits the use of his arms and hands, Art pedals his hand-operated tri-wheel wheelchair from Salt Lake City to St. George, Utah, setting a 335-mile world record. This guy is "wheelin' and dealin'" with life better than most "able-bodied" people I know.

Hmmm... a marathon. Could I do something like that?

I pay little attention to his speaking business. I don't see myself as a speaker, and running a business of any kind seems way beyond me. But these other things he was doing catches my attention. If he can do such things, well, I don't know that I can do all that... But maybe... I have to try something. Anything to get out of the house.

Family life now revolves around taking care of me. This is not acceptable. I need to take care of them. Shondell and our boys need a sense of normalcy and so do I. I am ready to move forward. I have to do something, somehow. I don't exactly know what I will do or how, but I need to get out of the house. I need to go to work and "bring home the bacon." I feel like *The Little Engine That Could:* "I think I can, I think I can." But I also feel derailed. Where do I go? How can I work? What can I do?

It is as though this whirlwind of thoughts creates a vortex that begins to draw in possibilities. My friend Lee Johnson steps in.

Lee and his wife Cathy have been close friends of ours for years. Lee is the general manager of Broken Arrow, a construction company. He asks me to help him out at his company – maybe do some clerical work or something. At this time, I can barely pick up a pencil, much less write anything with it; however, I agree to give it a shot. I don't know how I am going to do it, but Art Berg has inspired me to believe that anything is possible.

Lee's offer is hard to accept, though. Lee doesn't act like he is doing me a favor, but it still feels like charity. How could he possibly think I would be of any real help in a construction company? That's a world of trucks, lumber, cement, tool belts, muscle and sweat. How on earth could a quadriplegic fit in that kind of world with that kind of energy?

I have no idea.

This is one of my toughest life lessons – to learn to accept the kindness and generosity of others and move ahead with faith. I keep my doubts to myself. I swallow my pride – and humbly accept his offer.

I start immediately. Five days a week, Cathy picks me up for work. She helps Shondell transfer me to her car and then she drives me to the job site. When we arrive, Lee helps transfer me from the car to my chair and I push my way up the ramp he built for me to get into his office where I start work. When I say I start work in "his office," I mean it literally.

Lee is the head honcho, so he has the best office. It's right in front. I can't get up the stairs where the other office workers are, so Lee gives me his big beautiful office. I am flabbergasted. Talk about reasonable accommodation! He has no guarantees of what I can do, but he gives me a chance – and his office.

If I wasn't humbled before, I sure am now.

Here in my own private haven, I reacquaint myself with the world of business. I don't have much physical ability or strength. Even simple office tasks can be nearly impossible for a new quadriplegic. I hear Art Berg's voice in my head. "Chad, you and I can do anything anyone else can, if we are willing to do it differently." I hear my dad's voice saying, "Amen!"

There are so many things I cannot do. If I tried to write them all down, the list would stretch into next Thursday. But what if I shift my focus? What if I focus on what I *can* do instead of what I *can't*? I list what I have left rather than what I have lost. I come to realize that is a pretty big list, too. Family, friends, faith...

One thing I do have left is my voice – and it is getting stronger all the time.

Lee and I get together and make a plan. We focus on what I can do. I can handle the phones and a computer. With a little adaptive equipment – like the special gloves developed by my friends at rehab – I can dial the phone and handle a computer keyboard. I use a headset, so I don't have to use the speakerphone and sound like I am calling from a cave. This is my first job. Answering phones. Taking messages. I am a receptionist.

Like riding a bike, takin' care of business comes back to me fast. I begin by focusing on simple clerical tasks at hand. I keep in touch with customers. I learn to listen, serve, take care of daily details. My responsibilities are fundamental, my contributions simple. I arrive at work on time and with the right attitude. Anyone can do that. Not everyone does. Every day, I do all the little things that help businesses large or small survive and then succeed. Because of Lee and Cathy's faith in me, and their willingness to give me an opportunity, a transformation takes place almost instantly. I am a breadwinner again.

Maybe Lee is not an expert on hiring the handicapped and accommodation and all that, but Lee saw something in me that I think a lot of businessmen fail to see in the disabled.

He saw me.

He saw Chad.

He didn't see a broken fellow in a wheelchair. He saw someone with something to contribute, even though, at first, he didn't know what I could contribute. At Broken Arrow, I didn't feel broken. I didn't feel different. I felt like a member of a team. I responded accordingly. I used every bit of the drive and focus I used in building my own business and running my ranch into serving my friend. I do things. I get things *DOne.*

Sometimes, if you really pay attention to who you are hiring – the *person* you are hiring – and accommodate their difficulties, and do so not out of pity but because you respect what they have to offer, such as the perseverance and creativity they have developed while dealing successfully with their difficulties, you give yourself the gift.

Opportunity is Lee's gift to me. Dedication, focus, and loyalty are my gifts to Lee.

At Broken Arrow, I rediscover something I thought I had lost; something vital for my future and the future of my family. I rediscover my confidence and my ability to run a business. Because of Lee's faith in me, I reinvent myself as a contributing human being and a working professional. I am a husband and father, providing financially for my family.

I develop great relationships with Lee's regular customers and start to get outstanding bills collected. I don't see myself as a collector; I am just developing relationships and getting people to honor their commitments. I surprise Lee, and myself, by bringing in a $15,000 debt that had gone uncollected for several years. Lee turns collections over to me entirely and also puts me in charge of sales.

Every time I give more, I gain more. I already have Lee's office; now I get my own secretary!

Then something happens that gives me new direction and purpose. Lee asks me to speak during our Christmas luncheon at Broken Arrow. I didn't know what to say, so I simply told my story. I guess they like my stories, because the CEO heard me speak and asked me to speak to all five hundred employees. He assigned me to speak about taking initiative, dealing with challenges, and doing all you can with all you have. I spoke to forty employees at a time during intimate luncheon meetings every Wednesday. It was fun. It was challenging. It started me thinking.

Small opportunities can lead to big things if we are willing to do the little things that are needed to get big things *DOne*. With a lot faith from my employer, and a little adaptive equipment, I return to the land of the living. Because of my employer's faith in me, I am again the breadwinner and a husband and father. Now I understand my dad's challenge. I *can* be happier, more productive, and more successful than ever before. I can run a successful business. I can be a husband and father. I may have to do everything differently, but I can do everything – and get it *DOne*.

Several months later, I am asked to speak a similar message of encouragement at a church meeting. Afterwards, a member of the congregation asks me how much I would charge to bring his employees the same message. I have no idea. I never really saw myself as a speaker. Can I do it? Could I even become a professional like Art?

I begin to dream again.

I call my mentor. He insists that I can do this, and do it well. He takes me with him to speaking engagements. He shows me how to better connect with my audiences. He shows me how to get real and communicate from the heart. He brings me into his office and teaches me how to build and manage my own speaking business.

Art Berg, mentor to millions, became my personal mentor and still is – from the other side. February 12, 2002, five days after returning from a trip to Hawaii with Shondell and me, Art Berg, age 39, dies unexpectedly in his sleep.

I am stunned. Art has given me hope and inspiration. He has been my anchor and the wind in my sails. Now, this incredible man, this man who blew into my life like a summer storm, is just as suddenly gone.

At Art's funeral, I sit quietly amidst the slow swirl of mourners. I wonder why so many precious things are taken from us just when we appreciate them the most.

"The Lord giveth and the Lord taketh away..." This just doesn't make sense. Yet.

About the Author

The Wall Street Journal calls Chad Hymas "one of the 10 most inspirational people in the world!"

Chad inspires, motivates, and moves audiences, creating an experience that touches hearts for a lifetime. He is one of the youngest ever to receive the Council Of Peers Award For Excellence (CPAE) and to be inducted into the prestigious National Speaker Hall Of Fame.

In 2001, at the age of 27, Chad's life changed in an instant when a 2,000-pound bale of hay shattered his neck leaving him a quadriplegic. But Chad's dreams were not paralyzed that day – he became an example of what is possible.

Chad is a best selling author, president of his own Communications Company, Chad Hymas Communications, Inc., and is a recognized world-class wheelchair athlete. In 2003, Chad set a world record by wheeling his chair from Salt Lake City to Las Vegas (513 miles).

Chad's speaking career in the areas of leadership, team building, customer service, and mastering change has brought him multiple honors. He is the past president of the National Speakers Association Utah chapter and a member of the exclusive elite Speakers Roundtable (one of twenty of the world's top speakers).

As a member of the National Speakers Association, Chad travels as many as 300,000 miles a year captivating and entertaining audiences around the world. He has graced the stage of hundreds of professional and civic organizations including Wells Fargo, Blue Cross Blue Shield, AT&T, Rainbird, IHC, American Express, Prudential Life, Vast FX, and Merrill Lynch.

Chad Hymas
Speaker, Author, CPAE
P.O. Box 187 Stockton UT 84071
435-843-5707
info@chadhymas.com
chadhymas.com
facebook.com/chadlhymas
@chadlhymas
@chadlhymas

Team CH

Embracing Moments That Matter

by Colleen M. Cook

THE PINK AND purple balloons attached with duct tape were a dead give-away that the young father had made the poster himself. "Welcome to summer vacation with Daddy, baby girl!"

As I and hundreds of others got off a long flight and made our way down the busy corridor of Salt Lake City International Airport, many of us noticed the sign, smiled and pointed it out to the others. The "WELCOME" at the top was big and bold, but the letters got smaller and smaller to ensure that all the words would fit on the poster before he ran out of space. As I hurried on my way to the airport baggage claim, I smiled and thought, "Oh, how awesome!"

I was grateful to be home from a long speaking engagement trip, yet something prompted me to stop, turn around and go back. I knew all too well that this, for better or for worse would be a moment in time worth watching, and perhaps I might even capture it on a cell phone camera. This father-daughter reunion scene was one that I did not want to miss.

So, I returned to the gate to find the father alone, anxiously awaiting the arrival of his daughter. I stood out of the way, but nearby to watch. The young man, casually dressed seemed out of his element with the hustle and bustle of the busy airport. He held the airport security's 'responsible party' paper in one hand and the poster in the other. He bobbed and swayed around the people, anxious and emotional, to get the first glimpse of his daughter.

As I watched quietly, my mind was flooded with feelings and memories from my own childhood. Throughout my growing up years, my parents were married and divorced several times, both to each other and to other people. I know this life and I know it well.

I recalled the many times when my younger brother and I flew from Los Angeles to San Diego for a weekend visit with our dad. We even earned our "golden wing" pins from American Airlines and got to take pictures with the Captain. That was fun, but I also recalled times of fearful confusion. Once, my mother put us on a plane to Salt Lake City to send us to grandma's house only to have my father arrive 3 days later and fly us back to L.A., this time with a restraining order.

Hard times for all to be sure. There were many challenging changes, new towns, new schools, and new friends—with several awkward moments. Like when it was time to meet Mom's boyfriend, or Dad's girlfriend. There were many hours wondering if our parents would ever get back together; wondering if we would ever be a family again. Or would we learn to make the best of this broken home, spending 'quality' time at Mom's house – then Dad's as the state of California deemed appropriate.

These thoughts raced back to my mind and heart as I watched and waited for this father-daughter reunion. I found myself wondering how old would she be. Would this be her first visit with Dad? Would she be a little girl accompanied by an airline attendant who had just given her a golden wing pin? Or would she be a bit older? A teenager, perhaps? Would she be excited to see her dad, or upset about being forced to spend summers with Dad as the court had ordered?

I pondered as I waited a few feet from the father. The thought came to me that this 'moment,' whatever it might turn out to be, would be one worth witnessing.

Passenger after passenger de-boarded and I could see the anxiety building in the father as he paced back and forth, standing on tiptoes to see around and over people as far down the gangway he could. Still, no one. No sign of the father's precious cargo.

That mother had better have put her on this plane, I thought, recalling experiences of my childhood. *Please*, I prayed, for that young father's sake, *please let her be next.*

After what looked like the very last adult passenger, the airline security people came through the door, leading several children. *Yes!* I thought, *she will be in this group for sure.* I watched as one by one, IDs were verified and the kids were connected with their respective adult. The excitement was so profound that I found myself holding my breath in anticipation. Finally, the look of anxiety on this father's face softened, his eyes filled with tears of joy and love, as he beheld his "baby girl."

Which one is she? I wondered. Then it became obvious. She was about 12 years old, tall and thin, with straight blonde hair and looked a bit like her dad. Tears flowed freely as they embraced and held on tightly to each other. How grateful I was to witness this beautiful moment. As they began to walk together, the father saw that I was ready to take a picture of them. He paused and motioned to his daughter to look at me. I knew instinctively what she was thinking. Who are you? Are you the new *girlfriend*?

I shook my head and said, "I am no one. I do not know you or your father. His sign caught my attention and it was just so awesome that I knew this would be a special moment and that perhaps I could capture it for you."

She smiled and I took a few photos and asked for his email address.. They each thanked me for my time and walked arm in arm to begin their summer visit.

I stood there, so grateful for the experience, for the prompting I received to stop my crazy-busy life for just a second and embrace a moment that mattered. My heart was full, and my life was enriched by this experience. All it cost me was a few minutes of my time. I could have so easily missed it.

The speed of life these days is one of our greatest challenges. The world often seems spinning out of control. Information flies faster and faster, requiring our constant response to keep up. Faster and faster we go, sometimes unaware of why we are hurrying and missing so much along the way.

In a favorite scene in the Star Trek Movie "Insurrection," a woman friend of Captain Jean-Luc Picard, Anij appears to slow down time. A waterfall becomes a magical display of beauty, a hummingbird's wings flap so slowly one can count the beats, and pollen blown from a flower floats softly in mid-air for the longest time. What an inspiring scene depicting what life would be like if we could control time. Of course, we can't. We can however, control ourselves, the speed in which we live our lives, and what we choose to do with our time.

I agree with these words from Mormon Apostle, Dieter F. Uchtdorf. "One of the characteristics of modern life seems to be that we are moving at an ever-increasing rate, regardless of turbulence or obstacles. Let's be honest; it's rather easy to be busy. We all can think up a list of tasks that will overwhelm our schedules. Some might even think that their self-worth depends on the length of their to-do list.

"The wise resist the temptation to get caught up in the frantic rush of everyday life. They follow the advice from Mahatma Gandhi. 'There is more to life than increasing its speed.' In short, they focus on the things that matter most."

Many of life's meaningful moments are so easily missed in the crazy-busy of our daily routines. It is helpful to recognize that we are ultimately in control. We are the creators of this "chaos." We have both the responsibility and opportunity to choose what we do with our time. The great thing is each of us gets to decide how often we choose to truly experience and embrace the moments that matter.

❖➤◄❖

Five years following the devastation caused by Hurricane Katrina, I had the privilege of speaking at a conference in New Orleans. There were many new buildings, streets, and parks with a stronger, more united, and very grateful city—

much more so that when I had visited many years before. Early one evening a friend and I walked through the old town and decided to stroll down a new walking trail along the Mississippi River. There were many quaint little shops, restaurants, and street vendors.

Between the sidewalk and the river was a patch of new green grass, cool and comfortable. The couple who occupied this spot seemed an unlikely pair. She was a bit older, with straggly grey hair, a dirty dress, and no shoes. She lay on the grass without speaking to anyone at all. The man, on the other hand, had on a nice button-down shirt, though a bit wrinkled, blue jeans and sandals. He sat on one of three overturned plastic buckets and with two beat-up drumsticks, drummed on the two other buckets. *He's actually pretty good,* I thought as I passed by.

My husband is a drummer and I felt it was only fitting that I put a dollar or two in the pie tin, which he had strategically placed on the sidewalk. The man stopped, and with his toothless smile said, "God bless you, ma'am." I smiled back, nodding, and kept walking.

Much to my surprise he stood and shouted, "Wait! Thank you ma'am. Please come back. Come back, I have something for you."

A little frightened, I wasn't sure what to do. I stopped. We needed to get back to our hotel, we didn't really have the time, and they were both a bit scary. But I called to my friend who had walked on and motioned for her to follow me. We turned around and went back.

The man smiled. "Thank you. God bless you."

I asked to hear his story.

He shared his plight. "My wife and I," he pointed to the woman sprawled out on the lawn, "lost everything in Katrina. Friends, family, our home, all of our possessions, and our livelihood. We migrated north for a few years and tried to make enough money to come home. We are now so blessed to be back. We are grateful for the mattress on the floor provided by a local church mission. It isn't much, but it is a start. We love this city and we are looking forward to rebuilding our lives here. To thank you for your generous tip, I would like to give you something just from me. I do not sing very well, but I will do my best." He rearranged his drums, picked up his drumsticks, took a deep breath and began to play "When the Saints Go Marching In." It doesn't get more real, more authentic than this. A seasoned gospel choir could not have done a better job!

On the banks of the Mississippi River, this grateful man sang with heart and soul. It was both inspiring and humbling. It was a moment that mattered to me and to him, and we embraced it. It is a memory I will forever hold dear. This was one of those moments that Maya Angelou was talking about when she said, *"Life is not measured by the breaths we take but by the moments that take our breath away.*" To think what I might have missed had I not stopped my crazy-busy life for just a moment to listen to his story, hear his song, and connect in such a powerful way.

As I have reflected back on this experience, I wonder if I should have snapped a quick selfie with him, or tweeted #homeless #Katrina #survivor. Maybe I should have recorded a video for YouTube, blogged the experience, or posted it on Facebook. I could have even created a "GoFundMe" page for him. At the very least, I could have sent an email or text to my colleagues who were attending the same conference to come and hear him play. I did none of those things.

What I have recognized since is that any one of these things would have detracted from that very special moment in time. I would have been worried about how I might look in the picture. Was the lighting right? Would the video sound be okay? Would it go viral? Would I misspell something in my blog or would my text interrupt friends? Instead, I chose to simply live life and be fully present in the moment. To relish the connection, to really soak it in and to wholeheartedly embrace a moment that mattered. I am so grateful that I did.

❯❯•❮❮

Atlanta 2012.

She had heard me speak once before and although I do not recall our first meeting, I will always remember our second. Before my presentation, one of the conference organizers approached me to let me know that there was someone in the audience who wanted to talk with me. I told her I would be more than happy to chat with the audience member. That was of course, after X, Y, Z. I wondered who this audience member was, what she wanted, and why she had the conference planner ask permission.

As the event drew to a close, I noticed a lady hovering in the hallway near my book-signing table. Though with some trepidation, I was looking forward to talking with her.

The crowed thinned and she came forward to introduce herself. "I know that you probably don't remember me, but I heard you speak three years ago at a similar event."

"Oh yes?" I said. "It was a great conference, wasn't it?" That is all I could think of to say. I remembered the event, but really did not remember meeting her.

She continued. "At that time, my life was in chaos. I had suffered several painful losses. I was unwell, depressed, discouraged and to be totally truthful," she paused for a moment and choked back the tears, "I had planned all of the details and was prepared to take my own life later that night. I don't know what prompted me to go to this meeting, I was not feeling up to it, but I went anyway. While I enjoyed your speech, it wasn't what you said on stage that had such a profound, life-changing effect on me. It was what you did afterwards that made all the difference. There were a lot of people around and much to my surprise, you approached me and said, 'You seem distraught; are you okay?' Though I had said nothing to you about what was happening in my life, somehow, you sensed my grief. I responded with very little about what was really going on, but you were kind enough to take time to talk to me. You even gave me a copy of your book, one that I could not afford for myself. I know now you were a God-send. It was clear to me that someone did care and that perhaps I would be all right. I am here tonight just to thank you for the time you spent with me, for your encouraging words, and for the hope you re-instilled in me. It was that moment that changed the course of my life."

As professional speakers, we understand what a privilege it is to have people's attention. We have the remarkable opportunity to motivate, inspire, and encourage people. Sometimes our words become a catalyst for positive life-changing decisions. But the lesson I learned from this dear lady was that she was not moved by my platform skills, my entertaining presentation, or my book, but rather by my willingness to offer a few moments of my time to connect with and care about her personally. Richard Moss said, "The greatest gift you can give another is the purity of your attention."

Lesson learned.

Time and time again, we learn that the most memorable experiences of life come when we are willing to slow it down, take time to truly connect, to love, and to serve others. I am grateful for these opportunities. My hope and my challenge to you is that you will choose to slow down from time to time and embrace the moments that matter.

About the Author

An enduring inspiration for over 20 years, Colleen Cook educates, motivates and celebrates audiences world-wide. Her positive enthusiasm encourages people to recognize their extraordinary potential and embrace all possibilities through personal accountability and principle centered living.

Colleen is the former host of the radio show, "Obesity's Surgical Solution" and the author of the internationally acclaimed, bariatric best-selling book, **The Success Habits of Weight Loss Surgery Patients.** Her company, Bariatric Support Centers International leads the bariatric support community, assuring optimal outcomes for those who struggle with the effects of the disease of obesity.

She is the founder and former chair of the National Support Group Network an Integrated Health Committee of the American Society for Metabolic and Bariatric Surgery. She has served on the National Advisory Board for the Walk From Obesity and currently serves on the Membership Committee for the Obesity Action Coalition. In 2009, Colleen was named "Bariatric Professional of the Year" by the Bariatric Care Network, and recently received *International* honors for her research.

She has been a member of the National Speakers Association since 1996 and has served on several local and national boards and committees, serving and inspiring her colleagues. Colleen's programs have been implemented in countries all over the world making her a sought after international speaker for both public and professional events.

Colleen M. Cook
President, Speaker, Author
801-898-4212
cmcook59@gmail.com
http://colleencook.com/
facebook.com/cmcook59
twitter.com/cmcook59

Colleen Cook
AN ENDURING INSPIRATION

The Art Of Significant Relationships

Twelve Truths To Creating Self Love, Attracting Intimate Connection, And Guaranteeing Your 'Happily-Ever-After'

by Dan Clark

"The individual's most vital need is to prove his worth, and this usually means an insatiable hunger for action, wherein he develops and employs his capacities and talents through love, admiration, and genuine interest in the life of another."

—Eric Hoffer

THERE ARE TWELVE Fundamental Truths that transform every relationship from successful into significance:

1. Successful People Get What They Want - Significant Individuals Want What They Get. Successful people begin with the 'end' in mind, focus on a destination that's impressive, effectively manage people to do things right, and reward results to get what they want. In contrast, those of us who are striving to achieve the level beyond success and live lives of 'significance,' begin with the 'why' in mind, focus on a journey that's important, efficiently manage expectations to inspire one another to do the right things, and reward effort to make sure we want what we get.

To illustrate: a teammate of mine was a second-round draft pick into the National Football League. However, after only four superstar years in the league, he walked out of practice and quit, never to play again. Why? He loved being a professional football player, but he hated playing football. He got what he wanted but didn't want what he got! He loved the money, fame, and celebrity perks that afforded him a successful existence, but because he was misaligned with his inner voice and purpose, he could not live a significant life, and would die with his music still in him.

2. Practice Obedience. In my book The Art of Significance – Achieving The Level Beyond Success *(Penguin 2013),* I teach the Twelve Highest Universal Laws of Life-Changing Leadership, while illuminating that the universe was organized by a set of irrevocable laws, the first and foremost being Obedience. All other governing principles and laws are subject to it.

In order to create our own life experiences and test our obedience we were given our free-will agency to choose.

To guarantee our agency we were given an opposition in all things: darkness to appreciate light; sickness to appreciate health; justice to appreciate mercy; death to appreciate the sanctity of life.

Because our Creator knew we would constantly struggle with our choices, each of us was born into the world with an inherent ability to discern truth from error and know right from wrong. We commonly call this 'intuitive north star' our Conscience. Which means our conscience will never fail us – only our desire to follow it decreases as we continue to do the wrong thing. Which means we will never have a temptation we are unable to bare, when we welcome the strength and comfort of our 'still-small-voice' that continuously reminds us to obey.

When we obey a specific law, we reap a specific reward and response that conform to that obedient action. When we disobey a specific law, we realize and suffer a specific consequence to that action of disobedience.

Sometimes we are tempted to measure our progress by looking at what others are choosing to obey, do, or have achieved. But our path is unique to us. If we choose to take detours, then we – you and I – and only you and I can find our way back. This particularly applies to relationships. Why?

Because of the way some use their agency they lose their agency. When we don't obey universal laws or the specific rules that derive from them, our opportunities are reduced, and we fall captive to our choices. However, when we do commit to obey, our obedience ultimately protects our agency.

Therefore, free will isn't quite as "free" as it seems – at least not from the point of view of significance. Without agency, you could not choose rightly and progress; yet with agency you can choose wrongly and fall short of your potential as a human being. Let me explain with my 'Parable of the Kite':

Parable of the Kite

A father and his young son are in a park flying a kite, when his dad asks him what holds the kite up in the sky. The boy answers, "The wind." Dad explains, "No, the string holds the kite up in the sky." Confused, the boy argues, "No, the string holds the kite down." Smiling, Dad says, "If you think so, let go of the string."

Obviously, when the boy let go of the string, the kite fell from the sky. As the wind blew the kite wherever it decided to, the boy chased the string until he caught it. When he grabbed hold of the string, the kite again climbed skyward to be everything it was meant to be and do everything it was meant to do at the highest level possible.

The *Kite* represents his (our) desired results - high expectation of an extraordinary forever relationship.

The *Wind* represents opposition including debt, infidelity, alcohol, drugs, untreated depression, self-centeredness, and thinking 'me' before 'we.'

The *String* represents the rules, every governing principle, the 'Five Love Languages,' and each of the Twelve Highest Universal Laws that he (we) must follow and obey in order to control our 'Kite Dream/Goal,' which is to create, maintain and enjoy an awesome relationship" from being blown and carried about by the winds of opposition and change, so he (we) can achieve the desired result.

The boy *Holding Tightly To The String* represents him obeying his dad (you and I) because of his/her position, persuasion and expectation.

The boy *Letting Go of the String* represents him (us) succumbing to the enticements of our materialistic world and the temptations of others, and experiencing the consequence of disobedience as he watched the kite blow away (and we see our most important relationships fall, fail and run away).

The boy *Chasing the String* represents him (us) following his conscience and realizing that when he only exercised Obedience to his Dad (or caved in to the persuasive powers of an unacceptable enticement) it was easy to rationalize disobedience.

The boy *Once Again Holding Tightly To The String* represents his (our) realization that we should never obey a person, because they will eventually let us down. Because the boy now has first hand experience in suffering the consequences of disobedience, he decides to exercise his free will agency and chooses only to obey the laws and rules that will lead to a perfect, solid relationship - not because it's expected by his dad (or our spouse or significant other), but because it's demanded of himself.

When our 'kite' is a healthy, significant forever relationship, regardless of the influence, temptation or distraction (person, persuasion), we hold tightly to the 'string' because our beliefs don't make us a better person – our behavior does. The string of rules that controls your 'Forever Significant Relationship Kite' includes a commitment to:

- F.A.M.I.L.Y. – Forget About Me I Love You!
- C.H.A.N.G.E. – Come Have Another Necessary Growth Experience.
- Honesty.
- Total Fidelity.
- Mutual Respect and Support.
- Daily Effort to make it work.
- Positive Attitude.
- Unconditional Love to always put the other person first.
- Laughter and Fun created in an official 'date night' one evening each week!

3. Find Your Personal 'Why.' I played American football for thirteen years until a paralyzing injury cut short my career. I was paralyzed both physically and emotionally for fourteen months and told I would never get any better. Have you ever heard this? What if you believe it – especially when it comes to your desire for better relationships? You and they will never get any better!

I stayed paralyzed because I was asking the wrong questions – asking the doctors 'how' to get better, when I should have been asking myself 'why.' Once we answer 'why,' and it truly is our own personal why, which makes it bigger than any 'why not,' figuring out the 'how-to' becomes clear and simple – not easy, but obvious.

No, this is not a raw-raw 'you can if you think you can' remedy. It is a biological fact based on the physiological proof that when we have a clearly defined 'why' coupled with a compelling 'want' (which is a passionate goal), our head and heart actually connect to increase the flow of blood in our veins, fire the brain and engage our muscles. When we only identify a 'what' and 'how' no such emotionally stimulating experience occurs. This is why reason leads to conclusions, but it is emotion that leads to action!

To transform our relationships from successful into significant, which means we want what we get, we simply need to ask ourselves at the beginning of every day 'Why am I with this person? Why am I married or with this significant other?' Once we answer 'why,' figuring out how to stay married, together and deeply in love (for the next hour and day and week and month and year – one moment and day at a time) will be clear and simple – not necessarily easy, but obvious with a commitment to do whatever is required to make the relationship work, grow, strengthen and endure.

It is my experience that every one of our personal 'whys' are generated by our level of self-worth and understanding of who we believe we really are, illustrated with an experience I had as a keynote speaker at a national convention.

The meeting began with the CEO speaking to his 5,000 employees. Suddenly a young, vivacious woman sat down next to me on the front row. I asked what her name was and what she did? With a big smile she said her name was Yolanda and that she was the 'Administrative Assistant' to the CEO speaking on stage. When he finished, Yolanda was invited to the stage to sing the National Anthem.

Amazing! Breathtaking! Before she had even finished the song, the crowd began to cheer and continued to cheer and stomp and whistle and clap for at least two minutes afterward. Truly she had blown everyone's mind, and people commented, 'As good as Whitney Houston" and "better than Beyoncé.' She finished and I was introduced.

So, how did I start my speech? I asked the crowd, 'Is Yolanda an Administrative Assistant who happens to be a phenomenal superstar performer, or is Yolanda a superstar performer who happens to be an Administrative Assistant? Who are you – really? Everybody else is taken!

Finding your personal 'why' is requisite to identifying who you are, and only when you connect the two will you have the confidence to be vulnerable with another, and the inner strength to do whatever is required to develop and maintain a 'significant relationship!'

4. We Become The Average Of The Five People We Associate With The Most.

When we hang around with five negative, whining, broke people we will be negative, whining and broke. (Miserable being finds miserable being – then they are happy!) When we put a hard to catch horse in the same field with an easy to catch horse, we usually end up with two hard to catch horses. When we put a sick child in the same room with a healthy child, we usually end up with two sick children. To be positive, disciplined, healthy and significant, we must be willing to pay any price and travel any distance to associate with positive, disciplined, healthy, significant human beings.

In order for them to want to associate with you, remember that the goal is not to be a person who needs a significant someone – the goal is to be a significant someone who an extraordinary person needs; who reminds us of the magnificence of both loving him/her as our equal partner and respecting our relationship as a character, chemistry, cause, commitment driven team. When we put the other person on a pedestal and ask, 'what is best for you and most significant to us?' our love grows, we validate that we are needed as we serve each other, and our relationship forever endures. And when we are a part we always say, *"I like me best when I'm with you, I want to see you again!"*

5. We Don't See Things As They Are – We See Things As We Are. When two people look out the same window at the same storm and one exclaims, 'Horrible,' and the other proclaims, 'Wonderful,' the weather did not change. When you get yourself right, the world is right. The goal is not to engage with everybody who wants what you have. The goal is to engage only with those who believe what you believe, so they choose you, not just someone who does what you do.

To illustrate, let me introduce you to a super smart, beautiful, twenty-year old woman who is an extremely talented and successful songwriter in Nashville, Tennessee. Consequently, the lead singing "bad boys of the band" are attracted to her, and she has fallen captive to the celebrity attention. To some fathers this is no big deal.

However, her caring and conservative dad, knowing the probable collateral damage of such fast and furious friendships, has continually counseled her to make sure she knows the end result is tied to the beginning choice. To his dismay, his fatherly advice fell on deaf ears, and his precious daughter continued to date the prima donnas until her dad spoke from an epiphany he had experienced.

He compared his daughter to a dog chasing cars. If the dog caught the car, what would she do with it? Although she got what she wanted, would she really want the 'sex, drugs and rock and roll' lifestyle that often leads to moral decay and relationship destruction? In this "aha moment," his daughter changed her probable future by seeing through a different lens and making a wisely informed choice.

Obviously her choice came from the illumination of what matters most, which is what lasts the longest, which triggered a desire to realign her inherent core values with the good, clean, pure, powerful, positive influences in the world that would inspire her to become more of who she really is.

6. 'Great' Is Not Always Good Enough - 'Best' Is Only Relevant Depending On What You Compare It Against. Are you tall, short, wide, thin, fast, slow, smart, stupid, successful or unsuccessful? Says who? Compared to what? In a conversation about anorexia and bulimia the doctors and therapists usually refer to these predicaments as 'eating disorders,' yet they have nothing to do with food. If you put a young lady on a deserted island with no access to fashion magazines and the photo shopped pictures of twiggy models, would she feel insecure and think she had a large bone structure or that she wasn't pretty enough or good enough?

If we played in a charity golf tournament and par for the 18 hole course was 72, and I shot 108, and yet you and everybody else shot 120 and above, and I win – I only win because I suck less than you suck! That's a bad system! I don't want to be the best dad in a room full of dysfunctional fathers. I don't want to be the best and top sales professional in a company of low achievers. If you are the smartest person in the room you are in the wrong room.

Bottom line. We must always be the authentic best version of ourselves - everything we were born to be – we will make a lousy somebody else. You are unique and special, and supposed to look the way you do. You are the snowflake that is clearly different from every other flake falling from the sky. Your DNA and thumbprint are so unique they will convict you in a court of law. You are supposed to be here on earth at this time for a specific reason, and are beautiful and magnificent just the way you are!

7. 'Hope' Is Not A Method – 'Faith' Without Works Is Not Faith At All. Too many are living their lives hoping to be happy, but because they only hope, they never really are. They are waiting for someone to ask them to the senior prom and have never even taken the time to learn how to dance. Finding, attracting and creating meaningful relationships is much like fishing, where in order to catch a certain kind of fish you must go to the lake where that fish hangs out, fig-ure out what that special fish is 'biting' on and attracted to, and then work hard for as long as it takes to catch the fish and take it home. Some just want to catch any fish and consequently continuously change their lures to attract whatever is swimming by. However, some stay true to doing what is necessary to catch only the fish they want and believe they deserve! You can pray and think and believe and 'hope' all you want that the fish is going to swim up your street and hop in your boat, but it's never going to happen.

Those who sit around philosophizing if their glass is half empty or half full have missed the point. It's refillable! Thinking positively or negatively doesn't fill up the glass. The pouring does! It's easier to act our way into positive thinking than to think our way into positive action. It's not the sugar that makes the tea sweet – it's the stirring.

Some devout religionists think it's only about 'believe and be saved.' No. It's about entering into a joint venture with God to do whatever we can to help the Almighty answer our prayers. Too many go through the drive through and order a Big Mac, large fries and a huge Diet Coke, and then have the gall to offer a blessing on the food praying that 'it will strengthen and nourish their bodies and do them the good they need.' Seriously? Too many gather at a school for a multi-car caravan drive to a vacation destination, and the 'hopeful' and 'faithful' ask someone to offer a prayer who pleads, 'Bless us to arrive safely that no harm or accident will befall us,' only to have some get in their vehicles and drive 100 mph without wearing their seatbelts. No, no, no! God will not be mocked!

8. Self Is Not Discovered – Self Is Created. To attract the right person we must first be the right person, by seeing ourselves in a positive light that includes who we are *and* who we have the potential and power to become.

For example, if you are overweight and negatively see yourself in the mirror as a fat failure, you are sabotaging your chances for success with a pessimistic attitude toward change. However, when you positively see yourself as someone who has been very successful at putting on weight (ha!), you will realize that you gained it one pound at a time and therefore, can lose it one pound at a time! Bottom line: when the things we think deeply about are different than the things we do, we will never be happy.

This is where the 'art' of significant relationships begins to unfold. The 'science' of relationships is a step-by-step process most famously referred to as our 'Love Languages,' which according to marriage counselor/author Gary Chapman, is categorized into five primary ways in which we emotionally communicate and understand love from another: Words of Affirmation, Quality Time, Receiving Gifts, Acts of Service, and Physical Touch.

The 'art' of significant relationships, however, is created and maintained when we emotionally communicate and understand the love we have for ourselves. In other words, before we can like and love and trust and honestly communicate with another, we must first like, love, and trust ourselves!

Too many compromise and give up what matters most, which is what lasts the longest, for what they think they want at the moment. They sell out to get a job that they really don't want to do just to be employed; they party hard and contradict the personal honor code they've been raised to believe, just to be popular instead of respected; and because they connect with someone when they are not being authentically real and at a lower point in self esteem and moral conduct, this new found relationship is based on fantasy instead of fact.

When they tie the not, which usually resets their desire to live in personal integrity and congruency, aligning who they are with what they do, because one of the two in the relationship was not true to him/herself in the beginning, and he/she decides to change and personally grow and improve and take life to the highest level that he/she deserves it to be, the relationship quickly collapses and ends in heartbreak. Ponder this as I invite you into my junior year at East High School.

Selling Out

Her name was Jillene Jones. She told me it was Portuguese for 'awesome woman' and she was right. She was wonderful! I wanted to go out with her more than anything in the world. I was somewhat insecure and didn't want her to turn me down, so to protect my heart and ego, I asked some of her friends if she would go out with me. They all said yes. I got my confidence up, practiced my voice to make sure it was low and breathy, and phoned her. I asked her to a concert two weeks away. She said yes!

My plan was to get her to fall in love with me. I didn't think Jillene could possibly like me just the way I was, so I started asking around to find out what she did like. I was willing to change anything about myself to get Jillene to fall madly in love with me. I was willing to sell out and compromise my personal authenticity just to reel her in.

I spent the next fourteen days researching Jillene. I discovered her favorite color was peach. What a drag. Peach is a popular color now, but in college it was definitely uncool for a guy to wear peach. You just didn't do it. But it was Jillene's favorite color. I wanted her to fall madly in love with me. Suddenly, it was my favorite color. Interesting how that works, eh? And no, I didn't just buy one peach shirt - I bought five peach shirts. I was thinking long-term relationship!

More research revealed Jillene's favorite men's cologne - an exotic-sounding substance that stunk so bad my nose hairs threatened my life. When I splashed it on, my eyes fogged up, my ears tried to bleed, and my eyes started to sting! But it didn't matter. It was Jillene's favorite cologne. Suddenly it was my favorite cologne. No, I didn't buy the small, date-size bottle. I bought the huge forever-relationship-size bottle. It cost me a bloody fortune!

I did more research and discovered Jillene's favorite music. I liked all kinds of Self-Worth music, but hers was really different. Heavy, heavy metal - brutally loud stuff. Sometimes I think the only reason they call it heavy metal is because the lead singer sounds like he dropped something heavy on his foot! And to think they wrote this all by themselves! Whoa! Give them a Grammy! Yeah, I bought a CD. Suddenly, heavy metal had become my favorite kind of music. It's interesting how insecurity works.

Two weeks went by. It was finally date night. It was time to take Jillene to the concert. I took my research seriously and put on a peach shirt, drenched myself in the cologne, and went to pick up Jillene. I stunk so bad that the flowers on her front porch began to wilt. Jillene answered the door, and all my preparation paid off. "Oh, my gosh! I can't believe it. Nobody wears peach. Peach is my favorite color." She gave me a hug.

"Oh my gosh," she continued, "this is my favorite smell - my favorite cologne." I coughed and choked, "Me too. I can't believe how many things we have in common." She smiled and said, "I know, I know."

I walked her to the car, opened her door, and walked around the car gagging for oxygen. I then popped in the CD and played her favorite song. As we pulled out of her driveway she leaped over the console and started singing (or screaming) to the beat, and head banging up and down in heavy-metal contortions. I joined her, nodding my head up and down until I accidentally hit her nose on my forehead.

As her nose started to bleed, she yelled, "Wow, you're a great slam dancer. This is my favorite band." I yelled over the loud music, "Me too!" We pulled onto the street and headed for the concert.

Jillene fell madly in love with me exactly as I had planned. In fact, she fell in love with me for two weeks. But something happened. I got sick and tired of being Jillene Jones. I was born to be me! I was born into this world to discover myself and become a unique person that I could love and respect twenty-four hours a day - every day. And yet I had just sold out to win over a woman! And how many women sell out to win over a man? We change our hairstyles, health habits, high expectations, moral standards, style of clothing, cologne, and tastes in music just so an individual or some cliquish group or club will welcome us and accept us with open arms.

After two weeks, I got sick and tired of being Jillene. I was born to be me. So, I gave the peach shirts to my sister. I threw the cologne away. (My trash cans smelled so badly every dog within thirty miles of my home had brain damage!) I then got rid of her musical noise and started listening to my own tunes. I even started doing the old favorite things I had once enjoyed. And do you know what? It turned out Jillene Jones didn't like that me. When I finally started to be real, we were completely different and she didn't like me. But that's okay because I like me. Do you like and love you and trust yourself? If not, why not? And if when, why not now?

9. We Attract What We Believe We Deserve. What you think about and believe in is what you attract. If your desire is to attract positive people and positive opportunities, you must be a positive person creating positive opportunities. The Law of Attraction is no secret. It's been around for thousands of years and is similar to the Law of the Harvest in that we reap only what we sow - input equals output 100 percent of the time.

The fundamental governing principle of the Law of Attraction is 'Likes Attract Likes.' You are a magnet, attracting everything to you, and this unfathomable magnetic power is emitted through your thoughts. Every one of us puts out measurable energy that falls into a specific frequency that can only be felt by someone on that same frequency. Are you putting out positive or negative energy? Look around. Are you attractive or unattractive?

If you don't like your current program and the vibe you're obviously dialed into, finely-tune who you are, tune-in to your true frequency, and start sending that energy out! One wavelength, one frequency, one signal and one vibe can only attract the same wavelength, and same frequency, signal, and vibe. "Likes Attract Likes" is a principle of the universe that never changes for anyone or anything.

To illustrate: Imagine you're driving down the winding road of life tuned into your program of choice, and for some reason you lose your connection. Instead of continuing on and frantically changing your channel to settle for a subpar shallow, temporary program fix that is easily found and commonly heard, why not stop? Eliminate the distractions that are blocking your reception. Go where you can hear, feel, and fully experience and easily tune back in to the frequency and deeper, meaningful program that you enjoyed before. It is there. The program is always broadcasting. But it is our responsibility to find it and tune into it!

When it comes to the Law of Attraction we must never think it's a "build it and they will come" proposition. Obeying the Law of Attraction means we are always bettering ourselves to be more interesting and appealing, and actively searching for the individuals who share this same passion, purpose, and desire to connect with us. When our energy guides us to each other, our frequencies perfectly match up, our communication vibes are strong, and the signals we are transmitting and receiving from each other are coming in loud and clear, it is beautiful at home, at work, at play, on a team, in a business deal, in a military squadron or platoon, in community service, and especially in the arms of our "one and only!"

Regardless if it's a personal or professional relationship, our feelings are a feedback mechanism to us about whether we are on track or not, whether we're on course or off course. Of all the questions you may have, the most important to be clear about are, "What do I want? What is possible to achieve? Do I actually believe I can get it with my weaknesses and limitations and strengths? And, do I believe I deserve it?"

Honestly answering these inquiries is fundamental in creating and projecting our chosen energy force, wavelength frequency, and continual energy flow. To simplify, let's talk about the process of purchasing an automobile. The first question is: do you deserve to drive a new car or a used car? Whatever your choice, you immediately notice others driving similarly conditioned cars.

I decided I deserved to buy my dream sports car. I was in Hawaii and paid good money to rent a red Ferrari. What a joke! I removed the coupe hardtop to make it a convertible, and the windshield came up to my chin. My head stuck out the top and I looked like Mr. Potato Head! I had to duck to drive and couldn't even get it out of first gear!

After much searching, I finally discovered a Porsche that had plenty of head-room and I decided that I deserved to own and drive one. What happened when

I got "clear" on what kind of a new car I was going to buy? I suddenly started noticing how many cars were like mine on the streets and highways. A guy at the end of my street drives a Porsche and until I knew what I wanted, I had not noticed his car before.

Then I got clear on the style I wanted and focused my energies on buying a 911 GT3, fuel injected and turbo-charged with a whale-fin on the back. And do you know what happened? I was blown away by how many 911 GT3 Porsche's there were with a whale-fin on the back there were in my community.

Greater Clarity Creates Better, Deeper, And Quicker Attraction

I got even clearer and decided it should be charcoal grey. And what happened? Although there weren't a lot of them on the road, it was amazing how we seemed to find each other. In one week I saw five other cars exactly like mine. In fact, one night I pulled into the left hand turn lane at an intersection and a Porsche that looked exactly like mine pulled into the left lane across from me. It was instant brotherhood. He flashed his headlights, so I flashed mine back. He flashed them again and I flashed them back! We threw down hand fist pumps and exchanged smiles to acknowledge what we had in common and then drove away.

Isn't it interesting that this Law of Attraction also holds true when it comes to belief? When you have become clear on what you believe, it is obvious that you automatically attract others who believe as you "believe. Positive finds positive - miserable being finds other miserable being, then they are happy!

The same thing holds true for someone who thinks they only deserve to drive an old beat-up used car. They pull into the left hand turn lane at an intersection in their rusted-out 1977 Buick Skylark with a broken muffler, a bad air shock and the two-toned paint chipping away. Sure enough, another 1977 beat-up Buick pulls into the left hand turn lane facing them. Just like with a new car, it is still instantaneous brotherhood as the guy flashes you his one headlight. (Ha!) You flash your one headlight back, and together smile with that look, "Yo Dude, what up with government programs? Represent homie!"

Obviously this analogy has nothing to do with socio-economic conditions. It is a tongue-in-cheek illustration that 'likes' truly do attract 'likes.' Remember, the goal is not to just get what you think you want at the moment. It is to want what you get so you don't die with your music still in you. Which means if you don't like what you're attracting, change what's attracting it!

10. Become An Artist Of Communication. Research shows that the quality of your relationship is directly related to the quality of your communication skills.

Notice I didn't say 'quantity,' but rather 'quality,' which means that you talk about things that really matter. It means that you are not afraid to express what you really think and feel and that your partner trusts you the same way. When you are in an intimate relationship you need to feel understood and accepted for who you are, so in the unconditionally loving arms of your partner you know you are safe to open up physically, intellectually, spiritually and emotionally. This in turn invites and reassures your partner that he/she can do the same, as you implement my six ways to create intimate communication:

- Share thoughts and feelings with each other without fear.

- Pay attention to your partner and be sensitive to their needs – physically, intellectually, spiritually, emotionally, socially, financially and with their own family members.

- Eliminate every reason and scenario where your partner might feel jealous, insecure and possessive.

- Choose the right words (what you say and should not say in phone calls, writing verses in person).

- Express the right body language (constant eye contact, never turning away from your partner, nodding your head in agreement, showing that you are listening).

- Touch in the right ways, in the right places, at the right times (hugs, holding hands, gently stroking the back of the head and arm, whispering in the ear, sexual intimacy – never with a domineering attitude and always with mutual respect and common consent).

And… let us never forget that the #1 cause of a breakdown in intimate communication is **Pornography,** defined as: 'printed or visual material containing the explicit description or display of sexual organs or activity, intended to stimulate erotic rather than aesthetic or emotional feelings.' Pornography desensitizes you to a mindset and heart set past the point of feeling that often leads to isolation, secrecy, and deceit that damages relationships by creating unrealistic expectations and conditioning us to see people as objects to be used and abused.

Let's face it – a porn star has a perfectly sculpted silicone filled body created by a plastic surgeon who specializes in T & A, and as a professional sex machine, has moves and stamina that none of us have. It is unacceptable and unfair for any of us to be compared with such fantasy creatures! And when we can't measure up to the pornography that our partner has been watching, we lose touch in the bedroom, and disconnect in the family room.

Accurately discerning whether or not an individual is struggling with pornography is difficult, but there are a few signs you can look for. While just displaying one of these signs might be a poor predictor, the more that are present, the more concerned you may want to be:

- Loss of interest in sexual relations.
- Denial behaviors such as defensiveness, rationalization, minimization.
- Neglect of responsibilities.
- Increased isolation with late-night hours on the computer.
- Emotional withdrawal from family; critical of spouse and children.
- Easily irritated; irregular mood swings.
- Unexplained absences.
- Unexplained financial transactions.

Bottom line solution: One day I was flying cross-country with my ten-year old daughter, when in the middle of our card game I asked her to hold her cards up closer to her face so I couldn't see them. In response she scowled at me and blurted, "Just don't look!" Any questions? Am I going too fast?

11. Make 'Commitments' - Then Establish 'Covenants.' A 'Commitment' is a two-way contract born out of suspicion, where you make a list of your responsibilities and I'll make a list of my responsibilities. I will hold you accountable and you will hold me accountable. If either one of us default and refuse to fulfill any one of our line item responsibilities the contract is nil and void. A 'Covenant is a one-way promise born out of trust and love, so no matter what you sat to me or how you mistreat me I remain the same ethical, honest, unconditionally loving person I have always been. I don't love you because of who you are. I love you because of who I am! For this reason, love is universally relevant expressed in contexts as diverse as married life, everyday work, school and athletics.

To illustrate: Successful people settle for the preparatory principle of selfish romance and believe that love is a feeling. Significant individuals live the advanced, highest law of Love and Be Needed, which they know is a commitment. If I love you because you are beautiful, that's romance. If you are beautiful because I love you, that's real love - a love that inspires each of us in the relationship to become everything we were born to be. Consequently, each and every time you leave the presence of those you really love, the authentic richness of this love compels you to say, "I like me best when I'm with you, I want to see you again."

To love is to give unselfishly of ourselves, fulfilling others' needs, and in the process proving to ourselves that we are needed. When we know we are liked and loved but don't believe we are needed, we withdraw from the very people giving us love and the familiar places where we usually find it. We stop engaging ourselves in the togetherness of life by declining connection with others, which creates thick, reclusive barriers with those we claim to love - all because of a thinning feeling of not being needed.

Individuals who are journeying beyond success and into the dimension of significance deliberately choose to avoid entangling themselves in what are called codependent relationships, where, individuals need others in order to *survive.*

In codependent relationships the successful spend their energy just trying to hold on and to survive their counterfeit happiness and pretended success. The significant make wiser choices and take control of the opposition in things by creating interdependent relationships, in which the parties *need others to thrive.*

Mere romance can devolve into lust, but love brings out the highest, noblest parts of our being, enabling us to experience life to the fullest and to realize our purpose as human beings. An unwavering commitment to unconditionally love and give more than we take, prompts us to continue to bring out our best even after we've reached the pinnacle of conventional success.

Being Needed

With this complete understanding of love, it is time to take your relationships to the highest level of interaction, commitment, and service before self. Love is not the answer - it's the assignment! However, once you show and tell, and live, and demonstrate your love to your most significant others, the highest law of loving is to be and feel genuinely Needed. This is when, where and how we transform our 'Commitment Action Love' into 'Covenant Service Love.'

I learned this fundamental truth in the 1980s when I was the main professional speaker in President Ronald Reagan's White House who took First Lady Nancy Reagan's "Just Say No" positive-choices school program nationwide.

While speaking to millions of teenagers at thousands of high schools in all fifty states, I became deeply involved in the suicide epidemic that was sweeping across North America. Plano, Texas, saw six suicides in the same day - seven in the same week. I conducted special programs to help communities deal with suicides in New Jersey, Utah, South Dakota, California, Florida, New York, Vermont, Massachusetts, and Connecticut.

In Iowa, one hundred suicide attempts took place within thirty days at one high school. One girl died. The school brought in Charlotte Ross, a national consultant on suicide, and me to talk to kids and families, where they gathered with counselors, school administrators, and health-care professionals to interview each of the students who had attempted suicide.

To my surprise, the students all explained that they wanted to give up on themselves and on life because they lacked commitment relationships. We have already established that love is a two-way commitment, and therefore, "I love you" are the world's three most powerful, two-way commitment-oriented relationship words. However, the world's three most powerful one-way covenant service-oriented words are "I need you."

These students told Ms. Ross and me *they knew they were liked, they knew they were loved, but they didn't believe they were needed. And when we don't feel that we are needed, why hang around?*

For example, one of my friends decided to get married. He asked if I would write a song and sing it at his wedding. I said no. He proceeded to remind "me that we were best friends and that it would be cool for me to participate in his special day. He basically made me feel important. Everyone likes to feel important so I finally gave in and wrote the song. Two days later, he phoned back to explain that the band had just canceled, and he wanted me to prepare forty to fifty songs to play as the dinner entertainment. I emphatically said, "No way!" He countered with, "I need you." Had he said, "I love you," I would have responded, "I love you too - here is the number of a band."

But "I need you" made me realize that I was not just good, but that I was good for something - that I really mattered, that I could make a significant contribution. I couldn't turn him down, and most likely you couldn't have done it either.

When the wedding day arrived, I sang the song that I had written for the couple. But before I could sing another tune, the band arrived. There was a miscommunication. I didn't want to sing all night, anyway. I wanted to eat and socialize like everybody else, so I helped the band set up their equipment.

Now, think about this: When I arrived at the wedding reception, I arrived with the attitude that my friend needed me, and I would have stayed until four o'clock in the morning if necessary, because he needed me. I would have waited tables, mopped the floor, and contributed in any way I could, because he needed me. But the second the band showed up, I was no longer needed. We can fool others, but we can't fool ourselves. So I left the reception and went home.

Are you needed? If not, why not? And what are you going to do about it right now? In the corporate arena, when a sales champion or outstanding executive jumps ship to work for the competition, it is usually not about money. There's a good chance that person no longer feels needed where he is, so he goes where he does feel needed.

Most of us think outside attention and recognition motivate us. It doesn't, yet we emphasize it in our marriages, personal relationships, business contracts, and athletic endeavors. What we desperately desire is to be genuinely needed.

In contemporary American society, we can't afford to wait for someone to tell us or show us that we are needed. It may never happen. We could go for months before we experience this crucial validation. So what do we do? Give up, quit, kill ourselves? Most definitely not.

Who are we fooling to think that society has to give our lives meaning, purpose, and excitement? We bear responsibility to do something on a daily basis to prove to ourselves that we are needed. If you don't feel needed by your spouse or significant other, serve him or her more and get more involved in their lives to show your respect and support of what matters to them. If you don't feel needed at work, participate more, volunteer, and get involved on committees and event-planning boards. If you don't feel needed at home, participate more and get involved. If you don't feel needed by your children, participate more, get involved in their world, volunteer in their schools, host their parties at your home, stay in touch, and get involved in their friends' lives. If you don't feel needed in your neighborhood or world, vote, participate in charity organizations, give more than you take, and leave everything and everyone in better shape than you found them.

12. Comprehend The Myth Of 'Finding' A Soul Mate And The Reality Of 'Being' One. Contrary to pop culture, perpetuated by constant tabloid sensationalism of Hollywood love, finding your "Soul Mate" is not a reality. In the original definition, he/she does not exist. It is an ancient myth introduced to the world in The Symposium: a philosophical text by Greek Philosopher Plato dated c. 385–380 BC, wherein he examines love in a series of speeches by men attending a symposium or drinking party (a boy's night out!).

Although it has always been called the "Soul Mate Theory," intelligent, educated and sophisticated individuals have allowed it to find its way into mainstream thought, our love stories, and as a result, into "our psyches and the way millions of people view falling in and staying in love.

Make no mistake: I am not suggesting that a soul mate wanders the earth waiting for you. This myth, rooted in ancient Greek mythology, and epitomizing self-centered, narcissistic thinking, is a major destroyer of relationships.

To illustrate: In Plato's Symposium, the myth holds that humans had four arms, four legs, and a single head made of two faces. Because Zeus feared their power, he split them all in half, resulting in a perpetual ache of separation and a longing to regain the completeness by finding one's missing half to re-create the whole.

Although harmless terms like "my better half" and "counterpart" evolved from this thinking, another human being was not created just to satisfy your needs or my needs, just to make us feel complete. Yet many believe and pray that destiny will lead them to the "right one," freeing them from having to do the hard and honest work of selecting a mate.

Do you honestly believe that you need a Soul Mate in order to complete your "humanness" and become everything you were born to be? As a "split-a-parter" you have been exiled by the gods to spend your entire life searching for your missing/other/better half to make you whole. And the worst part about subscribing to the fantasy idea of Soul Mates is that because you believe your marriage was 'made in heaven/meant to be,' you immediately start taking your relationship for granted, expecting perfection in your spouse, thinking that everything in your relationship should immediately click, and that there won't be any challenges.

Consequently, when you have disagreements and your growing pains are lasting longer than expected, you start rationalizing that somehow you made a mistake and did not find your Soul Mate after all, which tempts you to immediately bail out of your marriage and walk away from the relationship for that reason alone.

When your relationship fails, you attribute it to not having found your Mr. or Ms. Right, cut your losses, get divorced, and return to your hapless quest for the one who, once found, will cause you to live happily ever after.

Soul Mates Are Not Born – They Are Made

If you think that marriage to your so-called Soul Mate will mean a life free from hard times and conflict, and assume that a partnership of two Soul Mates should be able to handle challenging times easily, you are not facing reality and are setting yourself up for failure.

This sounds disappointing - mostly to the 20- to 40-year-olds who are still single or already divorced. However, the older folks who have been married to the same person for ten or more years will tell you that once you commit to being married, your spouse becomes your Soul Mate, and it is your duty and responsibility to work every day to keep it that way.

My dad told me that he fell in love with my mom from the first moment he saw her. Nevertheless, had she decided to marry another, he believed he would have also met and fallen in love with someone else. For the record, my dad is eternally grateful that this didn't happen, but doesn't believe she was his one and only chance at happiness in this life, nor was he hers. There is not just one right person for you.

Theologian Spencer Kimball sums up what commitment to Love and Being Needed means when he said, "Soul Mates are fiction and an illusion; and while every young man and young woman will seek with all diligence and prayerfulness to find a mate with whom life can be most compatible and beautiful, yet it is certain that almost any good man and any good woman can have happiness and a successful marriage if both are willing to pay the price."

Ironically, when we pay the price we become Soul Mates, described by Richard Bach as "someone who has the locks to fit our keys, and the keys to fit our locks. When we feel safe enough to open the locks, our truest selves step out, allowing us to be completely and honestly who we are; and loved for who we are - not for who we're pretending to be.

Although it's not possible to be a Soul Mate, becoming someone's Soul Mate is still an extraordinary romantic experience that is worth pursuing, where you share your devotion to the love of your life, promising: "I will care for you physically and emotionally, and give my whole heart to you, telling and showing you everyday, anytime, anywhere, any way I can, that I love you; constantly yearning to spend more time together gazing into your mesmerizing eyes, feeling the warmth of your infectious smile, and hearing your soft, sweet, soothing, reassuring voice that inspires me to be everything I was born to be; never wanting to go anywhere without you; never caring what other people think about the two of us; and being there for you no matter what, knowing love is the world, the world is love, and you are the world to me."

In the modern sense, true Soul Mates share our deepest longings, sense of direction, and support our purpose in life. They have the potential to turbo-charge our unique gifts, by unveiling the best part of one another, so that no matter what else goes wrong around us, with that one person we are safe in our paradise.

Perhaps we can forgive ancient writers with ancient ideas (probably quite modern for their time) but 2,300 years later, it's time to wise up! Instead of listening to 2000-year-old dead men, and mindlessly hoping for our Soul Mate to miraculously show up in our lives, why not spend our precious lives and irreplaceable time working on being real Soul-Mate-Men and incredible Soul-Mate-Women, who will attract real men and incredible women into our lives. Let us fall in love for the right reasons and commit to paying the price each day so we can enjoy the prize of true Commitment Action Love and Covenant Service By Being Needed for time and all eternity!

To help you fully understand the residual benefits that come when you transform yourself, your life, and your organization from successful to Significance, and to prove that getting "clear" on what you want is the only sure way you will always want what you get, let me share the lyrics to two of my most popular songs:

Real Man

I need a man
Who knows happily ever after, is a day at a time proposition
A man who knows making love, is not a three-minute composition
It's a slow dance, full of romance, a walk on the beach in the sand
It's having a whole conversation just by holding my hand
He will stir deep desire, that sets me on fire, to be with him all that I can
No, I won't settle for anything less than a Real Man

A Real Man's strong in stature, firm in faith, and kisses slow
He sometimes cries, and when we hug, he's the last one to let go
He worships the ground I walk on, he's my biggest fan
There's nothing like being loved, by a Real Man

I need a man who knows honoring me, is a macho disposition
A man who knows I love you, is a more than words rendition
It's roses for no reason, secret love notes in my drawer
It's making me his equal though he always gets my door
He will never raise his hand to me, believe in who I am
Yeah I can be more than I thought I could be with a Real Man

He talks to me through touch, I'm swept away in every clutch
We're lovers, but we're best friends too - I like me best when I'm with you

A Real Man's strong in stature, firm in faith, and kisses slow
He sometimes cries, and when we hug, he's the last one to let go
He worships the ground I walk on, he's my biggest fan
There's nothing like being loved, by this Real Man
(Dan Clark copyright 2000)

Yes, romance is awesome and necessary when expressed in the context of true love! Of course I am not this man, and many have asked me how a 6 foot 5 inch, 240 lb. linebacker could write such a song? Did I somehow get in touch with my "feminine side?" Au contraire Mon frère. I simply decided it was time to connect the left side of my brain with the right side of my brain, and with whole-brain thinking I started engaging all of my senses and became more fully alive. To write the song I simply made a list of things I wasn't (ha!) and decided I could become them if I made a commitment to take myself to the next and highest level – not because it was expected by another, but because it was demanded of myself!

To a parent this higher level of commitment means, "Any male can be a father, but it takes a special man to be a dad."

Special Man

A little boy wants to be like his dad
So he watches us night and day
He mimics our moves and weighs our words
He steps in our steps all the way

He's sculpting a life we're the models for
He'll follow us happy or sad.
And his future depends on example set
'Cause the little boy wants to be just like his dad

A special man talks by example
Takes the time to play and hug his lad
A special man walks by example
The very best friend a growing boy ever had
Any male can be a father
But it takes a special man to be a dad

He needs a hero to emulate
He breathes, "I believe in you"
Would we have him see everything we see
And have him do what we do

When we see the reverence that sparkles and shines
In the worshipping eyes of our lad
Will we be at peace if his dreams come true
And he grows up to be just like his dad

Yes a special man talks by example
Takes the time to play and hug his lad
A special man walks by example
The very best friend a growing boy ever had
Any male can be a father
But it takes a special man to be a dad
(Dan Clark copyright 1985)

About the Author

DAN CLARK is founder and CEO of The Art of Significance Development Company – an international high performance communications and training firm; University Professor; an Award Winning Athlete who fought back from a paralyzing injury that cut short his football career; Adventurer; Gold Record Songwriter; and a New York Times Best Selling Author, who delivers customized, cutting edge keynote speeches and transformational programs on leadership, building winning teams, and creating a culture of excellence to entry level employees, emerging leaders, and seasoned executives.

Since 1982, Dan has spoken to more than 5 million people, in over 5500 audiences, in all 50 states, in 59 countries, on 6 continents, to clients including 200 of the Fortune 500 companies, world leaders gathered at the 'Festival of Thinkers' in Abu Dhabi, NASA, Super Bowl Champions, the United Nations World Congress, our AF senior military leaders at 'Corona,' and to our combat troops in Iraq, Afghanistan, Kuwait, Qatar, Africa and across the globe.

In 2005, Dan was inducted into the National Speakers Hall of Fame, and both Achievers Global and eSpeakers have named Dan one of the Top Ten Motivational Speakers In The World.

Dan has been published in more than 50 million books in 40 languages worldwide, has appeared on more than 500 TV and radio programs including Oprah and Glenn Beck, has been the feature story in Mayo Clinic, Entrepreneur and Millionaire Magazines, and has been recognized as an Outstanding Young Man of America in 1982, Utah Father of the year in 2012, and recently awarded the United States Distinguished Service Medal – the highest civilian award given by the Secretary of the Air Force, and the American Spirit Award – the highest honor in the nation given to one civilian each year by the U.S. Air Force Recruiting Command.

Dan Clark, CSP, CPAE
CEO; New York Times Best Selling Author;
University Professor; Hall of Fame Speaker
The Art of Significance Development Company
P.O. Box 58689, Salt Lake City, Utah 84158
1-800-676-1121
415-968-9326
dan@danclark.com
danclark.com
facebook.com/danclarkspeak

Doing Love

by Darren Johansen

DO THE RIGHT thing for others – always. Love them. That will be the right thing for you – always. Loving someone is about our ability to love, not about another's ability to be lovable.

Velcro. That weird, wonderful thing inspired by cockleburs. Those nasty, insidious little seed-things that stick tenaciously to dog hair – and your favorite wool socks. Today, Velcro is a convenient staple used by NASA and kids and moms and firefighters and skiers and dogsledders – and you and me. Velcro has been incorporated into our language as a metaphoric word for persistent stick-to-it-iveness.

What does Velcro have to do with love? The quality of our lives is directly related to the way we treat others. Velcro illustrates that amazing truth. Ask yourself, am I the soft flexible side or the stiff scratch side? Wait!! Neither side of Velcro is bad. If you think you are the prickly side, others see you as strong, dependable, and resilient. If you think you are the soft side people feel you care, are sensitive, and welcoming. Love and life, like Velcro, need both. In genuine love we use our abilities to enhance the ability of others.

Here, it is; a metaphor for "doing love." The kind of persistent consistent love that holds together the fabric of our culture, families, society, business. This kind of love is a choice – it's an action, not just an emotion. The quality and cohesiveness of our lives is directly related to the way we connect and relate to each other. When we truly love, we use our abilities to connect with and enhance the lives of others. It is something we do – not just something we feel. We persistently stick with it, until we consistently do it. Genuine, persistent, consistent love is doing the right thing for others – always – and, yes, that will be the right thing for you – always.

There was an intense discussion, in a friend's Modern Social Problems class in college. A classmate addressed the issue of whether it is right to have sex before marriage. After strong feelings were expressed by the class, both for and against, the teacher simply said, "I am not going to tell you whether you should or shouldn't have sex before marriage." What I recommend is that you ask a different and better question. Ask yourself, "Is this really love?"

Perhaps that better question should drive all of our decisions.

It is hours after curfew. Your teenager still is not home. You call. You text. You pace the floor. No response. You decide to call the police. Suddenly you see the lights of your teen's car as it careens into the driveway and screeches to a stop. Your child runs through the door. You have a nagging, edgy gut tension. Your child quickly hugs you and says, "Sorry I am late" and offers something in the way of explanation, but you don't hear because your senses scream, "Something's wrong."

He seems "off." His words are slurred. You can't tell if it's alcohol or other drugs – maybe a combination. You blurt out, "Are you drunk?" Your child turns and runs back to the car yelling, "You don't understand! You just want to control my life!" You hear the squeal of the tires as he guns the engine and races off. What do you do now? What does love tell you to do?

When I was eleven years old, my parents sat me down for "the talk." This was not about sex. I already knew about the birds and bees; I was a sixth grader, after all. Mom said, "Darren, if we ever find you with drugs, alcohol, or breaking the law, we will drive you to the police station and turn you in."

They were serious!

"What?" I protested, "I thought you loved me!"

Now that I have children of my own, I realize the words my parents spoke were proof that they understood the real meaning of love.

Do you think calling the police creates more problems when young people act out? They could be incarcerated; have a police record. They could be influenced negatively while in detention. But, if being held in police custody for a night will help them understand the natural consequences of their actions, would it be worth it?

Whatever you decide, do so from a position of genuine love and you will likely do the right thing, even if it is the hard thing.

Steph was a feisty young lady. One evening, as she was coming out of Kmart, she saw someone flip a cigarette butt out the window of his car. She politely called out, "Excuse me, excuse me sir?"

"Oh, no, here we go again," her little sister, Andrea, thought. Her big sister often treads in places where most would not.

The driver stopped his car.

Steph asked, "Sir, do you have an ashtray?"

"Yeah."

Steph picked up his discarded cigarette butt and handed it to him. "Would you put this in your ashtray, please."

Chagrined, he took the butt from her and drove away.

A week later Steph's mother took her and Andrea shopping. Steph was on crutches due to a surgery related to an illness which eventually took her life. She had a disability parking placard. There was a police car parked in the handicapped stall, so their mom had to drop them off near the entrance and find another place to park. As Steph and Andrea approached the entrance to the store, the officer came out with a shopping bag in hand.

Steph smiled, and said in a polite, but disappointed tone, "Those parking stalls are for people who need them – like me. Why did you park there?"

With all the authority he could muster, he said, "I got called here for an emergency."

Pointing to the bag in his hand, Steph asked, "a shopping emergency?"

The officer mumbled an apology, walked to his car, and drove away, likely never to repeat the offense again.

This public servant had forgotten for a moment his identity and his purpose to protect and serve. Steph's good natured invitation to a place of discovery and understanding illustrates the principle of approaching people and dealing with difficult or even embarrassing circumstances with love, real love. This isn't just about feeling love. This is about *doing* love.

Love is not eliminating consequence.

It allows for it.

Love is doing the best for others and that will always be the best for you.

Opportunities to *do love* come in many ways. An opportunity to do love unfolded on the side of a mountain. A group of scouts and their leaders – the scouts called the leaders "the old guys" – made up our twelve-man crew outfitted with fifty-five pound packs. We had slept on pads over rocks for the last five nights. This was the last day on the trail and the longest hike of the trek. We were tired and happy to be heading back to base camp.

Awaiting us was hot cooked food, real toilets, warm showers, and a camp cot, which would seem like sleeping at the Ritz Carlton. This would be the final day of a long trek that would earn us all a Fifty Mile badge. As I placed one foot in front of the other in a strange, plodding cadence, my mind drifted back to a conversation I had the day before with my "back of the line" partner.

Ron was the oldest of the "old guys." He had come on this trip because he felt it was the right thing to do. He was the ecclesiastical leader of the group. He felt it would be good for the group for him to be there. It was tough for him, though. It took stamina – sheer grit – for him to make it through. Each day took more out of him. When asked how he was doing, Ron would simply say, "I'm gonna make it."

Perhaps it was love that gave him his courage, his drive, his strength – or was it the other way around? Did he have to feel it first – or do it first?

Dr. David A. Bednar said, "The word 'love' is both a verb and a noun... we think we have to have the feeling – the noun – before we start doing love – the verb..." He declares that the more we *do* the verb love the more we *feel* the noun love. When two pieces of Velcro come together, that's the verb. The connection from them being together is the feeling. Ron's choice to go on this difficult trek with these much younger men, illustrates the *verb* love which later brought the feeling and connection – the *noun* love.

Loving someone is about our ability to love, not about another's ability to be lovable. It is not what they do or don't do; truly, it's about our ability to choose how we will respond to them. Holocaust survivor, Viktor Frankl, taught, "Everything can be taken from [us] but one thing: the last of the human freedoms – to choose one's attitude in any given set of circumstances, to choose one's own way." He chose not to hate his brutal Nazi captors. He chose to love them.

Love really is about us *doing* love. This brings depth and meaning to the phrase in ancient writ, "God is Love." What happens when we believe in a God that loves because this divine enlightened being chooses to – because it is God's nature to love – rather than loving us because of what we do or don't do? We gain the freedom to make mistakes and not feel fear. Believing in a Creator that loves in spite of – perhaps even because of – our mistakes, opens a door of possibility where we can love others as He does.

Learning to love as God loves requires sacrifice on our part. We give up something good for... well... something better. We sacrifice the luxury of judging others. We gain love, insight, understanding, peace, joy. That's a pretty good deal.

Do the right thing for others. Love them. That is also the right thing for you.

On the trail with the scouts, I had a light bulb moment – a plan that would bring rest to Ron's weary frame and create an opportunity for insight and growth for the group. We would disperse the contents of his pack – spreading his load among the others. When these young scouts shared his load, they would better understand love because they would be *doing* love. They would feel love – the noun – when they chose to do love – the verb.

The tougher the sacrifice, the greater the love.

The last day of the hike was the most difficult of our entire journey. (I guess we saved the best for last.) One of the scouts was unusually quiet. Something was wrong. I sensed pain in his every step. He adjusted his pack several times. He no longer was one of the "front of the line" dudes. He welcomed every stop. I knew he had consulted first aid stations today and the day before. When asked if he was okay, the answer was "yes," but the tone and texture was "no." You could see pain in his eyes and hear it in his voice.

Like Ron, he too wanted to go the distance. He wanted to know he could make it. As we stopped for water and to catch our breath, I unstrapped the tent from his pack and added it to mine. He apologetically expressed his concern that my burden would increase. I assured him it would be fine. You could hear relief in his voice as he thanked me.

We climbed on. Beautiful vistas came into view as we ascended to the highest point of the journey and paused to celebrate. From the peak, we could see the path ahead. It appeared to be easy – it was literally all downhill from there. Great!

What we thought would be the easy part – wasn't. What goes up must come down. Everybody knows that. What we didn't realize was that "down" was harder than "up" – much harder. The terrain changed severely as did the pitch of the trail and the last leg became the most challenging part of our entire journey.

We descended three thousand feet in less than two miles. This was the hiking equivalent of a free fall. I had done okay with the extra weight thus far; after all, when you carry fifty-five pounds what's another seven? As I made my way down Cattle Drive Gulch, I came to a deeper understanding of what it means to share another's burden. Sacrifice is good because it brings for the giver a deeper feeling for the receiver.

When we love, we do more in a meaningful way; in the end we feel something deeper.

When we sacrifice, we gain. Our capacity to love increases.

When we love, the load we bear may even feel lighter.

Love is a verb, sacrifice is an action verb. Remember, sacrifice isn't just giving up something; it's giving up something good – for something better.

It is "doing love." The result of doing the verb love is feeling the noun, love. When we realize the power love carries and that exercising love increases our ability to love – we do it.

Like Velcro, when we stick together we are unified, stronger, harmonious. We become one.

Alone we struggle, weaken, diminish, we become inferior and detached.

Simply put—We are better together than apart.

Love, is limitless, in supply and impact. When given freely, it lightens the world and brings joy to the giver. Remember, loving is about our ability to love, not about another's ability to be lovable. Do the right thing for others – always. Love them. That is the right thing for you – always. Our capacity *to love* increases as we *do love*. We *do love* because it works.

About the Author

How do we "Do Love"? By being Velcro. I'm not talking about sticky clingy-ness, I'm talking about stick-to-it-ive-ness, persistent connection. Love others whether or not it's convenient, whether or not they earn it. Loving others is about our ability to love, not about their ability to be lovable. When we love without condition, we always do the best for others – and that is always the best for us.

Are you ready to Do Love? Decades of experience have led Darren to a new view of love. Read Darren's chapter and you can have greater depth in relationships, peace and more unity.

As the owner of Johansen Counseling Services, Darren Johansen, LPC, LUTCF, has over twenty years of experience as a Relationships & Money Specialist. He is passionate about helping others achieve financially sound, peaceful lives by illuminating correct principles – *meaning principles that actually work!*

He has shared wit and wisdom on the platform to more than a hundred thousand people here and abroad: Utah State University, Utah Department of Corrections, Penn Mutual, Intermountain Health Care, NAIFA, Utah Valley University, Logan and Orem Institutes of Religion.

He is a leader in the Good to Great movement. Read his message. Invite him to speak. You too, can move from good to great in relationships and money management by living the principles found in Darren's chapter.

"Darren has a great ability, as shown in this writing, to teach in a way that is easy to understand and to incorporate into choice making and positive action."

—TL Davis

"Thank you Darren for helping me see how to 'doing love' is more than just saying or feeling love, it requires conscious action."

—DSL

"Darren's teachings on real love have given me a deeper sense of personal peace. I am more patient and kind with my spouse, children, and even drivers on the road. :) I have come to realize that love truly is about my ability to do the best thing for others!"

—AH

Darren J. Johansen
LPC, LUTCF
Relationships & Money Specialist
801-369-8702
darrenspeaks@gmail.com
darrenspeaks.com
facebook.com/darrenspeaks
@darrenspeaks1
darren-johansen

NATIONAL SPEAKERS ASSOCIATION

NSA

MOUNTAIN WEST
Idaho, Montana, Utah, Wyoming

Don't Just Build a Network, Build a Movement

by Devin D. Thorpe

IT IS WELL understood in network marketing that you've got to know your "why." You have to understand why you are willing to ask your friends, family and everyone else you meet to join you in your business. It's important because there will be days when you want to quit and you'll need a compelling reason to keep going in the face of challenges.

We all share an innate desire to make the world a better place, to love and be kind to our neighbors, and even to help other people in far off places.

If you combine these two ideas, you capture the essence of my message. You can channel your passion into a cause that others share and move your work from mere networking to building a movement.

Let's assume for a moment that your "why" is your six-year-old daughter with diabetes. She motivates you to succeed, to work when it's hard and keep going no matter what. She motivates you to eat a healthy diet and to feed her and the rest of the family one, too. Ultimately, your desire is to see her grow up healthy with all of the care and treatment she needs to be a normal adolescent and teenager, to have a great career, and a family of her own. You'd like nothing more than to remove the challenge of diabetes from her plate.

There you have it. There's your cause. Curing diabetes, in this day and age, is not some off-the-wall, loony bin idea. It is in the realm of possibility. But it won't just happen. The fundamental research that will ultimately lead to a cure requires funding today. JDRF is an organization that focuses its resources on finding a cure for type 1 diabetes, the kind that affects young children most often.

Everyone who knows you shares your desire to see your daughter grow up healthy and happy. Many of your friends know other people with diabetes and share a passion for its cure.

What if you could marry your passion for curing diabetes with your networking business? Just think of the money you could raise for curing diabetes.

If you could build an organization of 100 people willing to commit $100 each for curing diabetes this year, that would mean $10,000 for curing diabetes.

What if you could get 1,000 in two years? 10,000 in three? By leading a movement you create the possibility of not only building a successful business for yourself, but you also create the potential for making a huge impact on a cause you care about.

Star Throwers

You are probably familiar with—or perhaps tired of—the story of the star thrower. You remember the one with the little girl walking along the beach after a storm, throwing starfish back into the sea before they dried up and died. As she works her way along the beach a curmudgeon approaches and challenges what she's doing, arguing, "Why bother, you can't save them all." She replies inspirationally, as she picks up another one to throw back, "It will matter to this one."

That story teaches a powerful truth—that everyone matters. But it also leaves us to conclude the curmudgeon was right, we can't save them all.

In the original, literary short story told by Loren Eiseley, the plot unfolds differently. The first-person narrator of the story discovers a grown man on a craggy shoreline throwing starfish and other sea creatures stranded among the rocks by a storm the night before back into the pounding surf. The narrator visits with the star thrower to get a sense of his purpose, then returns to his home pondering what he's seen. The next day, he returns to find the star thrower back at work and joins him. In other words, we see the beginning of a movement. We're not left to conclude that we can't save all the starfish but instead that we just need more star throwers.

The Scourge of Polio

In the mid-1980s, there were about 350,000 cases of polio every year. In 2014, there were just 356, representing a 99.9 percent reduction over 30 years. The tally for 2015 looks to be about one seventh that of 2014 and 2016 seems destined to be the last year that anyone on the planet will ever get polio.

There are about 20 million people, mostly volunteers and low-cost health workers, in the developing world who are engaged in this effort. This is a global movement and it will result in the eradication of only the second disease in the history of mankind.

There are a number of lessons we can learn from the successful movement to eradicate polio. They can be applied to building a network marketing organization that doesn't just make you successful, but that will actually change the world for good.

The first lesson comes from my visit to India after the eradication of polio there, despite the fact that it was widely expected to be the last country on the planet with polio. When I visited with the septuagenarian and octogenarian members of Rotary who had been working on the eradication of polio in India for the past thirty years, they told me, "We didn't believe we could do it." I heard this repeatedly from people.

This is a powerful lesson for you. You don't have to believe you can change the world and become successful in your networking business, you just have to do the things that will change the world and make you successful. Put another way, you just have to start throwing stars.

Your Cause

It is important for you to choose a cause you care about passionately. Chances are good that your networking company is already aligned with a cause. If it speaks to you and fires your passion, look no further. It will be easier to incorporate that cause into your business because the company is already supporting you.

If that cause neither moves you to tears nor moves you to act, keep looking. It is better for you to support a different cause, to change the world, and be successful than to fail at your networking and fail to change the world.

If you want to build a movement around a cause, you want to be mindful of finding one that will speak to others as well. Your daughter's diabetes works because she's your daughter and you care about her. Your friends and family also care about her and they care about the other kids they know with diabetes.

You don't necessarily need to have a direct, personal connection to the cause. You don't need to have adopted a child from Zimbabwe to have a desire to help the people there. You may care passionately about building a movement to educate girls there simply because it is the right thing to do. Your connection can be as simple as that you were once a girl who loved to read.

Chances are good that if you are passionate about something, others will be, too—especially once you share your passion with them.

Now integrate your cause with your networking business. Pledge that you will give a portion, say 10 percent or $20 out of every check to your cause. By pledging a portion of all your future earnings to the cause, you link the success of your cause to the success of your business. You want to unify the purpose as much as possible.

Don't feel guilty for not pledging 100 percent of your income to the cause. Don't let anyone else make you feel bad about that either. No one can give 100 percent of their income away. You need to live. You need capital to fuel your business. Don't be afraid to keep some for yourself and your family.

Start Throwing Stars

Now that you've found a cause, it is important to start doing something about it. Your good work is infinitely more valuable to the cause than your good thoughts. No amount of you caring but not doing will overcome the challenges ahead.

Look for meaningful ways to engage with the cause. Most organizations need volunteers, advocates and activists. Find a role for yourself with the organization that makes sense.

One of the keys at this stage of the game is to be sure that what you're doing is making the intended difference. Look for evidence that the activities you're supporting are leading to the outcomes you want.

In the polio fight, there was an existing vaccine (two actually) that could be used to prevent the spread of the disease. The challenge was to get the vaccine into every child on the planet. That proved to be more difficult than originally anticipated.

If you can't find published proof that what you're doing is working with the effectiveness of a vaccine (remember, even vaccines aren't 100 percent effective), then look for new ways to attack the problem and prove that they work.

One of the key things you'll want to be doing at this stage is to be talking about your cause at every opportunity. Put reminders in conspicuous places in your life: on the fridge, on your car bumper, on your screensaver, etc. Use social media to spread the word so that all of your friends and family begin to associate you with your passion for the cause.

Build Support and Momentum

As you think about how to begin bringing friends into your cause and your business, you want to link those transparently in your efforts. Your friends will hate it if you invite them over to your house to learn about a cause and then spend most of an uncomfortable evening listening to you talk about products and compensation plans. Instead, invite people to your home to learn about how they can be a part of your social mission and how your networking business can help them do it with a new source of income.

When you invite friends to your home—transparently—to talk about your cause and your opportunity, be sure to balance the presentation effectively. Give them plenty of time and enthusiasm for your cause and balance that with enthusiasm for the business—both products and opportunity.

Focus the discussion of opportunity as a way to fund their financial support and commitment to the cause. Explain that you don't want any donations for the cause tonight, you want pledges of future income from the business instead, because that will be so much more money in the long run. Remind them that what you're offering is a way to fund the cause with new money. They won't have to give any of their old income or savings to the cause, instead you'll help them earn the money so they may join the quest to rid the world of one big problem.

As you grow your business, be transparent about your income and support for the cause. Tell people what you've pledged to do and do it faithfully. They will follow your example.

Try to engage your organization in volunteering and related activities. Our hearts and minds have a tendency to follow what our bodies do. Service creates a tremendously good feeling. Certainly, you've experienced that yourself. Think how powerful it will be to your organization to do service together, to share those positive feelings and build relationships of trust and confidence that will allow you to hang together even when challenges come along.

As your downline grows and contributes to the cause, create a reporting mechanism that will allow you to track the money donated to the cause by your group. Post that progress in a public place online so everyone can point to the impact you're having. Even a small organization of a dozen people pledging $10 per week to a cause will quickly find that it is giving material amounts of money over weeks and months of time. As the organization and momentum build, you'll see the tally growing faster and bigger than you might have imagined possible.

Track volunteer hours as well. Those volunteer hours can be as valuable to the cause as the money. If there is a way to track the impact, the number of people served and the outcomes they experience, that is great. For instance, if you are funding diabetes research, you might want to track the research you are funding and the impact of that research over time. If you are funding education for girls in Zimbabwe, you could track the number of girls you've funded. You might even try to identify the girls you've funded and track their progress through high school and college so you can see the impact on their lives. The organization you fund should be willing to help you with these measures. (If not, you may want to take your money to another organization serving the same cause.)

Give Yourself Time

It has taken 30 years to eradicate polio around the world—and we're not done yet! If you are going to do something that really matters in this world, it won't be easy and it won't happen overnight. If you stick with it, however, you'll find that your combined impact can far exceed anything you might have done alone even within a few years. Just be careful not to expect too much, too soon.

This is equally true for your business. If you want to create something that will have lasting impact on your family finances, you can't expect that to happen overnight. It will take consistent work over a sustained period of time. Network marketing is a wonderful business. It takes little startup or working capital. You don't have to carry receivables or inventory, and it can become profitable in relatively few months. Many startups in other industries take years to become profitable. Just don't expect to get rich quick. Focus on creating something sustainable with integrity and transparency. Be proud of the way you conduct your business.

Build Your Leaders

As your organization grows, you'll have less and less time for nurturing newly enrolled people. It will become increasingly important for you to build your leaders. They will be the ones contributing the most to your cause and earning the biggest checks for themselves. The help you give them will be leveraged to support your cause and build your income as well.

Don't just help them with the business, help them to increase their impact for the cause. Guide them to experience the passion and joy you feel when you give and serve so that they will continue both to build the business and support the cause.

One great way to support your leaders is to recognize them. When you meet with your organization, be sure to recognize not only the leaders who are doing well in the business but also the leaders who are doing the most for the cause. Focus on their impact for the cause, the lives they've changed and the good they have done. Money may be its own reward, but we all crave appreciation and recognition, especially for the good work we do.

As you recognize your leaders, be sure to welcome all your new recruits. Help them to see the potential for recognition in your organization for the work they do to support the cause.

The Endgame Strategy

In the effort to eradicate polio, the first ten years of this century brought little progress. The organizations battling polio continued doing what they'd been doing to make great progress toward eradication of polio, but progress stalled as they neared the goal line. Ultimately, they concluded that the effort required to reach the goal would have to increase. There would be no coasting across the finish line.

In a marathon, all of the training you do is not so you can run the first mile fast, but so you can run the last mile fast. That is when the rubber really meets the road.

As you work to achieve your networking and impact goals, you'll recognize the need to work harder and more effectively. Highly successful and impactful people are operating at a level that most of us fail to achieve. Network marketing provides a clearer path for that success than can be found in almost any other industry, but the same rules apply. Exceptional results will require exceptional effort.

As you build your organization, consider what it will take to reach the highest levels of success in your company and to drive the sort of impact you most want. Curing diabetes will take billions of dollars. You may be surprised at the level of contribution you can make to that effort with a large and focused organization.

There are three specific things to prepare in your endgame strategy:

1. Prepare for adversity. There will be challenges, both small and large. Some will be easily predicted, like having one of your leaders quit. Others, like an earthquake that disrupts your business or sets back the cause you've been supporting, will be difficult to predict. Prepare emotionally, financially and organizationally for whatever comes.

2. Build your organization. The impact you want to have and the sales success you seek, will require a much larger organization. You've got to identify new markets and new opportunities to pursue in order to gather the people you will need to have the impact you want. This will likely mean more travel, perhaps to new countries you've never visited before. And you'll need to provide a higher level of training to your new and upcoming leaders to help them replicate what you're doing and empower them to have a strong impact.

3. Make the big push. Achieving your impact goals will take more money and more effort than before. Set money aside for your endgame push to be sure that you're ready for the travel, the training, the coaching and leading that will be required to take your organization to its full potential. By starting to save today for your endgame push, you enable yourself to achieve more than you may dare to dream or even hope today.

You Can Change the World

Blake Mycoskie launched Tom's Shoes with the idea of giving away a pair of shoes for every pair purchased. He couldn't possibly have imagined the scale of the success he would have. That success came, in no small part, to his absolute commitment that he would give away the promised shoes. Because of his commitment, people trusted that he would do so.

Today, Tom's Shoes reports having given away more than 2 million pairs of shoes, funded education in Liberia, provided clean water, improved sight, helped mothers deliver healthy babies and prevented bullying right here at home. Blake is changing the world in a big way.

Your network marketing company has provided you with the same opportunity to change the world at scale. You can make a difference that you can scarcely imagine. Have the courage to start throwing stars today and you will change the world.

About the Author

Devin Thorpe was a finance guy until he realized life wasn't all about the money. As a new-media journalist and founder of the Your Mark on the World Center, Devin has established himself as a champion of social good. As a Forbes contributor, with 350 bylines and over one million unique visitors, he has become a recognized name in the social impact arena. His YouTube show, featuring over 600 celebrities, CEOs, billionaires, entrepreneurs and others who are out to change the world, has been viewed over 200,000 times, giving him a recognizable face as well.

Previously, Devin served as the CFO of the third largest company on the 2009 Inc. 500 list. He also founded and led an NASD-registered investment bank. After completing a degree in finance at the University of Utah, he earned an MBA from Cornell University.

Having lived on three continents and visited over 30 countries on six continents and with guests from around the world on his show, Devin brings a global perspective to audiences around the world, empowering them to do more good and make their mark on the world. These lessons also enable them to change their personal lives and to drive positive change within their organizations. His four books provide roadmaps to audiences on how to use money for good. His books have been read nearly 1 million times!

His leadership programs include:

- Adding Profit by Adding Purpose
- Building a Movement to Change the World
- Social Entrepreneurship: Impact for Profit
- Crowdfunding for Social Good
- The Power of Impact Investing

Today, Devin channels the idealism of his youth, volunteering whenever and wherever he can, with the loving support of his wife, Gail. Their son, Dayton, is a PhD candidate in Physics at UC Berkeley (and Devin rarely misses the opportunity to mention that).

Devin D. Thorpe
Champion of Social Good
Your Mark on the World Center
48 West Broadway, 1903N, Salt Lake City, UT 84101
801-210-2919
speaker@devinthorpe.com
DevinThorpe.com
facebook.com/devinthorpe
@devindthorpe
@devinthorpe
forbes.com/sites/devinthorpe

DEVIN THORPE

Lose the Wait Do it now!

by Karen Lindsay

A FEW YEARS ago, I had the opportunity to sail along the coast of Northern Europe. I wouldn't be a passenger on a luxury cruise ship. Quite the opposite, I'd be a working crew member on a beautiful "tall ship."

There are only a couple hundred of these massive sailing vessels in the world. They are the great-granddaughters of the sailing ships that brought my great-grandparents to America. I had learned to love sailing when I lived in Seattle. Now I had a chance sail on a tall ship, retracing the immigrant voyage of my ancestors.

Dad was an adventurer. Mom most certainly was not. She considered it her job to keep the home fires burning, her children safe. Brilliant, articulate, proper and calm, Mom rarely got upset. However, when she got wind of my intention to sail alone with strangers in Europe for several weeks, she blew into my home like an angry winter storm.

"Karen! What are you thinking! (This was not a question.) It's dangerous! You can't afford it!" She left, closing the door *very* firmly behind her. I sank into my couch, stunned. I'd never seen Mom react like this.

A moment ago, I was ready to set sail on a great adventure. Now, suddenly, I was adrift; alone on a sea of doubt. Yes, Mom was right, I suppose. I should wait until I could afford a trip like this. I sank deeper into the couch, weighed down by the burden of knowing that although I had accomplished many things, in essence, I felt like I wasn't enough. She didn't say that I should reconsider because of my weight, but, as I sometimes did, I interpreted her comments that way.

Mom had taken the wind right out of my sails.

I sailed anyway.

If I waited (for money, for approval, for a better physical condition), I would have missed the boat, and the opportunity of a lifetime. Missing the boat is the primary source of many of life's disappointments; and I was not going to let that happen. Not this time. It was time to *lose the wait*.

Once I decided on my dream, the universe moved – to get in my way. I barely made my first flight.

Arriving in LA, I bolted for the International Terminal. The meticulous fellow at the ticket counter said I was supposed to check in two hours prior to takeoff for any international flight. It was ninety minutes before flight time; therefore, I was, too late and could not board. I stood at the counter, waves of anger and disappointment washing over me. He noticed the tears welling up in my eyes, and asked what was wrong.

I explained that I was sailing a specific route in commemoration of my ancestors who had immigrated to America. Having to wait until the next available flight would mean missing the leg of the trip, which commemorated the journey of my Danish Great Grandmother, Karen Margrethe, whose name I bear.

Suddenly he leaned forward with light in his eye and carefully asked, "So this is a *pilgrimage* – of sorts?"

I caught his idea! "Yes, indeed, it is a pilgrimage in memory of my courageous ancestors."

He quietly escorted me around the barrier wall and helped me board the plane.

Clearing customs in Denmark, I caught a cab to the docks. We arrived to an amazing reception that seemed choreographed especially for me. Fireworks (something I dearly love) arched into the heavens and exploded with multi-colored fury over the tall masts of seven enormous sailing ships.

After a few hours of jet-lagged sleep – in my sleeping bag on a ship's bunk, I walked the streets of Copenhagen, Denmark, in the early dawn. These were my first baby step into my journey – my pilgrimage – of thousands of miles. Clutched in my hand was a map of the city printed from the Internet. I was searching for the Copenhagen Cathedral that enshrines Thorvaldsen's world famous statue "The Christus." I knocked on the church door and, sadly, found it locked. I was crushed. More tears. Someone tapped me on the shoulder and in heavily accented English asked, "Do you want to go in? We are not open yet, but I work here, and will let you in."

I spent a magnificent few minutes seeing this master sculptor's works, then caught a cab back to the docks, where I immediately boarded the boat and sailed off to continue my adventure.

It is well known that the English language delights in baffling anyone trying to learn it. Many words, which sound exactly the same, will have totally different meanings and spellings. Such is the case with the words: wait and weight. In my case, they are nearly interchangeable. I wait because the time isn't right. I wait because I don't have enough money. I wait because of my weight, and the feeling that I'm not enough.

"What is the weight that makes *you* wait?" Do you feel, like I did, that if you wait long enough you will somehow magically become enough to move forward? Or are you willing to *lose the wait and just do it now*?

The very first night, the seas became so rough that everyone aboard ship, *including most of the crew*, was sick – except for me and one older lady. A wonderful old sailor had taught me that if I began to feel disoriented or seasick, I should focus my eyes on the horizon. Calm would return. Focusing on the horizon works, even in the dark, even when clouds obscure the horizon. And, so it is with life.

Focusing on the horizon is like focusing on what we can do, rather than what we can't. Sometimes we spend our time "arguing with reality." Wanting things to be different than they are. We can allow ourselves to almost sink, drown in our lack, our "disability", so to speak. Or we can focus on the horizon, our ability to learn, grow, change, experience. Are our eyes focused on the horizon?

We sailed the rough waters of the North Sea along the coastline of Scotland and England. I was grateful for a steel-hulled ship equipped with modern navigation systems, a highly trained crew, and a medical doctor (who was also a working passenger). I was especially grateful for my Norwegian Wool sweater and modern waterproof gear. I wondered about my ancestors. How did they ever survive this? The North Sea was very rough, waves like nothing I had ever experienced. It was extremely cold—even when comparing it to sailing near Seattle in the winter—and it was August. The waves pounded the boat, bouncing it around like a cork.

Days later we were in England. BBC news alerted locals that the tall ships were in Hull (a port which my Great-grandmother Karen and other Scandinavian immigrants had passed through). There was a great festival, with music and fireworks. Thousands lined the docks to witness the majestic beauty of the boats passing through the locks and to wish us "bon voyage."

My thoughts turned to my dear little great-grandmother, Karen Margrethe. Her wealthy parents so strongly disagreed with her decision to immigrate to America, that they took her before a magistrate and disowned her, allowing her only a paltry sum with which to make her way. We can be sure they were not on the docks waving good-bye.

Maybe I needed to have experienced my Mom's uncharacteristic moment of disapproval of my trip to have even a tiny glimpse of what Great Grandma might have felt as she left home against her parent's wishes.

Karen Margrethe' did not wait until the stars were perfectly aligned. She left for America at twenty years of age, alone, unable to speak English, never to see her homeland or even to hear from her twin brother, the rest of her life.

As a young woman in the 1800's making her way to America alone, and building a life for herself required a heart and soul of incredible strength. Karen had no assurance that she would even safely reach America, but she did not wait. She did not wait until she could comfortably afford it. She did not wait until her parents supported her choice. Despite having problems with her hips and being a diminutive 4'7" only weighing 87 lbs., she did not wait until her body was stronger – she sailed anyway.

Karen Margrethe *lost the wait* and sailed into a sea of uncertainty.

A "square rigger" is a particularly beautiful and historically significant type of sailboat. Its sails are square or rectangular, particularly efficient for sailing distances powered by the "trade winds" as was the route followed by European immigrants to America.

To manage the sails – to furl or unfurl them – one must climb up rope ladders into the rigging. This task cannot be done from the safety and stability of the deck. In America, climbing aloft is a duty generally reserved for only the highly experienced, agile, professional crew members. For many reasons, including risk and possibly insurance requirements, this opportunity is not usually extended to those on a casual adventure.

I did, however, choose to take advantage of that unnerving opportunity. When I stepped on the rope ladder with one foot, the other foot moved in the opposite direction. After climbing for upwards of twenty-five feet in the air, on this web-like ladder, I climbed another ten feet, leaning back with my entire weight supported by my arms and feet like a spider. Then I had to scramble up over the edge of a flat platform sometimes called the crow's nest. (I don't even want to remember the climb back down). Did I mention that I have a fear of heights?

When I climbed the rigging of a ship named the Sorlandett, this feat of bravery landed my picture in the newspaper back home, the image and article transmitted via satellite phone from the deck of the ship.

I also climbed the rigging on Stastrad Lemkuile, a three-hundred foot Norwegian ship, with a one hundred and fifty foot mast. Each time I climbed, the boat was under sail. The motion in the rigging is amplified by the motion of the water. Despite my weight, I could not wait, or I would miss this opportunity. I had to accept that I was enough – right now. I had to *"lose the wait, and do it now."*

Hesitation, procrastination… waiting because the stars aren't aligned, because the time is not quite exactly right… waiting until you are old enough, rich enough, smart enough, big enough, small enough – enough! It is a universal problem. Its time, now, to *lose the wait* and sail past our limitations.

Thoreau said, "Most of us lead lives of "quiet desperation." Might this desperation be dissolved when you *lose the wait* and do what you desire to do – now.

When I talk about sailing, it sounds so beautiful, so glamorous. But I did it in the hard times. My adventures illustrate my point, but often they have come midst rough transitions, midst the challenges of life, and almost always midst a lack of resources, like time or money.

For instance, I began to sail because I had moved to Seattle for a job that a year later, laid me off. I embarked on what turned out to be the great adventure of learning about sailing by being a volunteer leader on a huge wooden yacht (sailboat) owned by the Boy Scouts (Sea Scouts). This ninety-foot wooden sailboat had been built for the Vanderbilts, used by the military during World War II (because a wooden boat was difficult to detect with the technology they had at the time), then donated to the Boy Scouts. They needed volunteer leaders, providing me an opportunity.

I chose to do something new (sailing) rather than sit stifled by the sadness and anger of losing my job. I chose something about as far from my childhood experiences of skiing, snowmobiling, and moving cattle on our ranch, as imaginable. I knew nothing about sailing, and still know very little.

Sailing can be an incredibly expensive but I was willing to volunteer hours of hard work (helping to refinish the wood on the boat was almost a constant project) to earn the privilege.

This is one of those times that I didn't *wait*, I sought out and opportunity to do something new, and did it *now*.

In 1995, I attended a university class, *At Home in Your Body*. The teacher asked, "If you could change anything about how the world interacts with you [as a large woman] what would it be?"

I quickly responded, "There would be snowmobile and ski clothes to fit me."

Her response is vivid in my mind, she said, "You really don't get it do you? Most other large women have given up [sports activities]."

That was a huge "aha" for me.

What she was telling me is that many larger women had bought in to a set of limitations that were now affecting all of us. She indicated that because they don't believe they can participate in sports there is no market for those clothing items. I wondered if that was true.

The memory of my awakening experience in class that night—is vivid—the realization that we can, and often do, allow our *wait*, to hold us back, to deny us some of the rich blessings of life. Of course I am blocked sometimes by my *wait* / weight. We all are.

Why was I so lucky as to not totally buy into some of those limitations? How did I dodge that limitation from totally blocking me from participating in skiing, snowmobiling, and other activities I've enjoyed? I'd love to pass on to you what I've learned from my life and study and observation of others, things that have made all the difference for me to *lose the wait*.

What did seem true was, while I was the only truly large woman in the room, each class member was carrying the weight of prejudice; a common belief that their body was not good enough. Their imagined weight was making them wait. I promised myself that I would continue to guard against letting that kind of belief keep me from actively participating in life.

In 2008, I was invited to go on a four-day white water rafting trip on the Green River. These canyons are so rugged and inaccessible that the famous outlaw, Butch Cassidy, hid out there. An experienced guide is required in every boat because they know every bend, ripple, and set of rapids, and help us safely navigate rough waters – as in life.

To run the rapids, to even be on the river, every participant is required to wear a specific class of lifejacket *and must be able to zip it up.* That stopped me in my tracks. I didn't want to plan and anticipate this trip with friends, drive to the Colorado outback, only to be disappointed and embarrassed – left out of the fun – because my size and weight wouldn't let me fit into the life jacket provided.

I didn't let my weight force me to wait. I called ahead. I asked the lady who answered if they had a lifejacket that would fit. She assured me that they had a very large lifejacket. To be absolutely certain it would fit, I asked her to measure it. Good thing I asked. Their largest life jacket was a full eight inches too small to fit around me and zip up.

People are great if you give them a chance. She was willing to accept the challenge to locate a suitable lifejacket for me. When I arrived, I zipped on the jacket with delight and launched into the rafting adventure of a lifetime.

I am so grateful I made that phone call and decided to *lose the wait and do it now.*

"A ship is safe in the harbor, but that's not what ships are built for." [Gael Attal]

"Twenty years from now you will be more disappointed by the things that you didn't do than by the ones you did do. So throw off the bowlines. Sail away from the safe harbor. Catch the trade winds in your sails. Explore. Dream. Discover." [Mark Twain]

Weigh anchor, Sail off into your dreams. When things get a little rough, keep your eyes on the horizon.

Lose the wait, do it now!

About the Author

Is there something you've dreamed of doing, but you haven't done it yet?

Is there something you envision for your organization, but haven't proposed or implemented yet because, maybe the time just isn't exactly right?

Karen Lindsay, Professional Speaker/Trainer/Facilitator for corporations, private groups and volunteer organizations, is your "Wait Loss Expert". She can motivate you and others to stop procrastinating – *Lose the Wait and Do it Now.*

Enjoy this article. It provides a preview of Karen's ability to share insights and tools that will help you understand more about yourself and rescue your organization from Someday Isle – that's [Someday I'll]. Invite Karen to speak.

Testimonials:

> Poet Robert Frost must have been describing Karen when he said, "[She] is not a teacher, but an awakener."
>
> —Thomas Cantrell,
> Administrative Law Advocates International

> Karen is a storyteller, reinforcing and illustrating her points with stories from her life and the lives of others. She gives participants practical, immediately useable skill sets."
>
> —Brad Barton,
> Nationally Recognized Keynote Speaker

What happens when you "Lose the Wait and Do it Now?" You enjoy life. You succeed on your terms.

When Karen "Lost the Wait" she...

- Sailed Tall Ships in the North Sea

- Enjoyed an African Safari

- Rode a Camel at the Pyramids of Egypt

- Sea Kayaked rough waters in the Strait of Juan de Fuca.

But this book isn't about Karen. It's about inviting you to *Lose the Wait* in your work, in your life!

Karen Lindsay
Speaker, Author, Coach
801-712-9633
Karen@KarenLindsaySpeaks.com
KarenLindsaySpeaks.com

NATIONAL SPEAKERS ASSOCIATION
NSA
MOUNTAIN WEST
Idaho, Montana, Utah, Wyoming

The Love Equation

by Leta Greene

THIRD GRADE MATH. If that sent a shiver up your spine, then you can relate. We were to pass off our multiplication tables and each of my peers in turn had done so. Only three remained. It was my turn—again. I am not sure, but I think they were tired of seeing me up there. I read into their stares and silence, echoing my own fear, my palms sweaty, stomach churning, panic building. I waited for number questions to be said and the awkward silence as I tried to pull from my brain knowledge that simply didn't stick.

You see I knew what I was…I was dumb. I had been told it in a thousand ways. No excellence here, look away folks nothing to see here, just another stupid kid that can't even do her multiplication tables! Let's add that to the list of failings that shadowed my young life.

2x2… that's 4…

5x6 = 30…

7x8…

I had nothing. Then from the second row one of my classmates mouthed, "fifty-six."

I repeated it, the teacher didn't notice. That's how I passed math. I cheated. Promising my young self that I would never ever stand in front of people again.

Hide.

Dumb.

Ugly.

I was only nine and had life all figured out. I received the message because my internal radar was programed to receive the signal it knew. I had added up the words, messages, and experiences and I knew the answer.

You have it all figured out too, don't you? What have you added up in your life to see yourself as limited? What have you believed without question? What do you know that you can't possibly do? When in moments of stress and hurt, do you divide away what is possible and minus away your potential? When a dream is before you, do you dismiss it knowing you are not in that equation?

Doesn't feel very good does it? How many times have you reached out only to assess that you are not worth it? In order to change your self-view you have to love yourself enough to change. No one else can evaluate the probability for you; our ability to assess others, to give to those in our radius, is only limited by our own self-determination. Seeing yourself as the least common denominator is missing the true formula of self-love.

By avoiding math, my knowledge didn't grow. Evaluating the variables and getting the correct angle not littered by your practiced routine will open up new paradigms. Don't cheat yourself and others out of seeing what you can do by adding up all the past. Divide out the negative and bring in what is congruent with a new variable to your math: Love.

In my book called "How to Embrace Your Inner Hotness," I share 15 steps to understand how amazing you really are. Today I am an international speaker, trainer, author and makeup artist. Most importantly I am happily married and have three of the best kids ever. Not trying to be a bragger. These are the facts.

I am an expert in all things Hot.

I am literally called Hotness. Really. The funny thing is you can't see me right now, so before you get an image of what you would define as the perfect woman let me stop you. You are adding the elements of what you term as hot, desirable and sexy. Let me share with you what I, Hotness, define as Hot.

There are two kinds of heat we put out. The kind that burns everything in our path like a wildfire burning out of control, leaving want and destruction. OR, in contrast, a campfire that draws others closer to it to feel of the comforting heat, to make s'mores, to share stories. And if you have ever read Jack London, a campfire will save your life. Per molecule, a campfire is hotter than a wildfire because it is contained. It is in control. Those rocks that surround it don't limit it but help it to burn hotter, safer, and most importantly help others with its light and warmth. Yes a wildfire attracts the nightly news. Most campfires go unnoticed on channel 5, but unnoticed to those around them? That quietly simmering campfire can ignite the spark that brings light to darkness, and brings hope to another, simply because it is simmering so safely next to you. I could share with you those who sparked my hotness. The interesting thing is that I didn't see their heat reaching out to touch me or to help me, because my perception of me was all cold. I saw only what I had programmed myself to see, as we each do.

As a newlywed I joked that I didn't have to know math because my hubby minored in math and majored in Electrical Engineering. He could do all the math for us. My kids do great at math. I got through those years where they asked me math questions, the home stretch. I was in the clear! No more math for the rest of my life. Freedom!

I couldn't help my kids with math because the numbers were not inside me. But I could love them, I could tell them that they were smart, I could give them acceptance, belief, and love because those are things I do have. **We can only give to others what we possess**.

There is this app on my phone called Math Puppy. If you get the answer right it dances and smiles. It is cute. My kids loved it. My finger hovered over it to erase it. After all my youngest is 10 and she has her multiplication tables down. She was past the dreaded stage. I had managed not to pass on my ineptitude. Except did you know that MATH NEVER ENDS?! It builds on one concept to the next. The numbers are everywhere; even with a calculator you can't escape them. They are all around us. We can divert our eyes and try not to see them; we can use tools to help us understand. Yet numbers are still there, never ending. There is always new and more! You literally can never stop counting. Look at that. The sheer mass, the multiplication of that and apply it to us, to all of us! We are seemingly just a number of all the people that have lived, live now, and will live, so how could just one person really matter? One of my favorite writers of all time, Dr. Seuss, wrote, "To the world you may only be one person; but to one person you may be the world."

You matter. You have heard this again and again. When we are hurting and scared we may be receptive to help like I was when the answer was whispered to me—but I came away feeling like a loser because the answer wasn't inside of me.

When changing what we add up about ourselves we change the equation and we get a different answer.

When we hear and see only negative, that is what goes into the result. Failure equals more failure, hurt equals being unloved—we have it all added up. So how do we change the algorithms of our internal calculations?

Just like numbers never end, neither does love. Love can be multiplied endlessly, but unlike math we can't define it by an equation with a definitive answer. We have to give it to feel it; we have to want to see it for the warmth of love to touch us. With ice cold determination we can turn it away and stand correct in our perception that it was never there. The justification of pain locking us in a place of cold existence—we call ourselves correct for knowing where things are. We have it all figured out. We know—just like I did at nine. It doesn't matter your age; we all have room to grow in adding love into our lives, the warmth of which will enhance every aspect of our life.

Here is one suggestion to help you increase the heat of love in your life. Start with your perception, what elements you are adding into your day. Start small with one thought that warms you.

No one else can do this for you.

Only you can put into your thoughts, repeatedly, what you decide to think about. When we start to count we start with one, two, three; we master that and then addition, subtraction, multiplication, division, algebra, calculus—each building on the last. If you feel your foundation of self-care is cracking at its base, start there, where pain is easing in, and add in a new statement congruent with truth. How do you find it? Truth is in us from the source of Love and you can feel it ringing true. It is our logic that strips it away. So start simple. I started with "Everyone in this room loves me." I repeated it once, twice; it pulled at my tongue tasting rough it was so new. The one variable clearly in my favor was that it was my own mind and privately in there I could say what I chose. You have the same factor of choice in you, so start.

Start with Vanity Prayers. It's my secret formula for subtracting the negative and exponentially increasing the positive. What are Vanity Prayers? We all have those moments when we look in the mirror and say mean things to ourselves. We focus on our scars and flaws, both internally and externally. Like affirmations, mantras and meditation, Vanity Prayers are designed to clear out negativity and focus on the positive in you. But they differ from your average positive thinking session because they require you to turn any perceived weakness or imperfection on its head. Vanity Prayers demand a new attitude from you—one that will change the way you see yourself.

The Four Steps to Using Vanity Prayers

1. Verbally (out loud) acknowledge specific strengths, talents, and good qualities you have.

2. Note the specific things you hate about yourself (this is key!). Then figure out what is good about those things. What do they show you about your power, worth, and the blessings you've been given?

3. Use these steps as a foundation to move through your day with purpose.

4. Develop a routine in the evening to review the day, acknowledge your honest efforts and treat yourself with kindness so you can peacefully have a well-deserved rest.

Choose to see the good adding up in you, just like you would your best friend. When your friend has a bad day, you tell her all of her great qualities. You encourage her, support her, and you are patient with her. When you look in the mirror, do you reinforce all the imperfections you see? Vanity Prayers will help you be your own loyal best friend. See your scars and imperfections in an entirely new and empowering light. Vanity Prayers will help you learn to change your tone and have a heart-to-heart talk about the changes you need to make.

In my youth I looked in the mirror and saw things I wanted to change because of what I heard society say about me. When I realized those things didn't add up and I improved my thinking, I saw that what was really wrong with me was not WHAT I looked like, but HOW I looked at myself. As I developed a forgiving heart and learned to laugh, something magical happened – I got prettier! When I improved my thinking about myself, I became prettier to others and myself. It is only when we connect with ourselves that we can give our best self to others.

Just like memorizing the multiplication tables takes practice, starting your morning with Vanity Prayers also takes diligence and repetition. It helps you start and order your day with the right attitude. Do it with the intent that you know what is coming in your day and you are prepared, knowing you are the person you were meant to be. Starting the day with Vanity Prayers is using the power of your own internal dialogue to set the tone for your entire day. Use it to rewrite your negative routine of self-incriminations, critiques, and comparisons.

What if those around you are not in your corner cheering? From their perspective you don't have much potential. They are naysayers, the "can't" talkers, "what more could you want?" Always negative, minus…not enough, will never be…oh, so depressing isn't? To see what cannot be! We have all heard, "show me your five friends and I will show you your life." Who you hang out with and who you listen to will impact the way you think. How you think will be the sum of your life—it's the equation of success.

I remember hearing this statement and looking around my life. Who I was related to and friends with, many who not only didn't believe in my potential, they also didn't believe in themselves. That lack of self-kindness spilled out onto me. I heard the words and they went deeply into my self-evaluation of my potential.

Could it be the same with you? That those around you who don't believe in themselves can't see you achieving either? Their math is off. They don't know how to add! Where we came from is not the sum of who we are. The voices you allow to be your self-talk will tweak your math to a positive or a negative each time; it is a variable in your daily life. One or two voices can be so negative that you equate their words with each step forward. Most say and do what they do out of no malice, just a general feeling of compromise and settling on what is now. Their habits are contributing to their words, treatment of others, and their perception of the world. You can be exceptional by what you accumulate between your ears. Start by changing what you add in there. But how?

Do you want more? More happiness, success, health, time, love, achievement, vacation, and spirituality? Not everyone is motivated by the same ideal. What motivates one person may have no appeal for the next. So how do you determine what motivates you? Look back and assess what has been a constant source of motivation. Is it relationships, connection, respect, status or self-improvement? It usually is not simply money. It is what you want that money for or what the money means to you. You may want money to pay your bills, to provide a better life for your family, or to vacation more. We each have our own end result. When you know what you want and why you want it, you will find the habits you need to create to achieve your goal. When your "why" becomes greater than your discomfort at doing something, the "how" becomes easier.

You don't feel you're adequate to reach your goal? Welcome to being the exception! Seriously though, there are only a unique few among us who failed to see that we shouldn't try. You may simply lack a needed element to your equation. Go find someone that can teach you what you lack, read up on the topic, and practice your new skill.

Think about those you admire, those you want to be like. Is it because they have everything handed to them? Life was easy for them and written out clearly? No, it is because they overcame something really hard; they had real odds against them. History shows us examples of heroes, victors, and visionaries. We are inspired by their stories. More impactful to us personally are those who are usually unknown in history, yet known to those they are near. They impact us by their heat of kindness, encouragement, support, mentoring, and love.

Everyone who has achieved something great has had friends, family, and neighbors that told them they were crazy. We all have people who see us in the same equation as themselves. Seeing only mediocrity in the mirror, it is improbable that they will see potential in others. Look to see what is possible and it will reflect back to you.

What great achievers have in common is their positive habits. In my training sessions I share about developing your five positive habits. Successful people may not all have the same habits, but they do certain things daily that are in line with their goals. Their formula for success is going to be different depending on what they want the end result to be. The CEO, the mom, entrepreneur, college student, athlete, the priest, will each have different daily habits needed to achieve their symmetry of success.

What five habits do you need to add? I think the first one is always Vanity Prayers—how you start to reprogram the talk inside you head. This will change how you bring in the world around you and what you spend your time focusing on and, as a result, what you begin to see as possible.

The biggest, scariest obstacle in our way, when we really assess it, is our own belief – or lack of belief – in ourselves. Do you really love you enough to put the work into you, to what you can achieve, what you can have in life? Or are you hiding the missing element of success—you. You are enough. You are no more or less than anyone else who has done great things in life. Olympians that have limps, people with learning disabilities who invent great things, the kid who is raised in squalor becoming a financial success, or the abused child who grows up to have a happy family. Others have overcome greater challenges than most of us face to become an inspiration to us—and so can we, so can you.

If you do not want to do your Vanity Prayers for you, then do it for those that love you. We can improve, we are all a work in progress; the final calculation isn't done yet. Love yourself enough to start.

Currently, I am working on my Sevens. The little math puppy dances a few minutes each day for me. It's very encouraging when I am wrong and it never whispers the numbers, or gives the answer to me. It's okay to make mistakes, to fail. It's part of the math of life to love yourself through your imperfections and see that they are adding up to make something really hot, amazing, and worth seeing as limitless.

About the Author

As a trucker's daughter, Leta, a.k.a. Mrs. HOTNESS™, has learned the ins and outs of the beauty industry from the outside in! She has learned them so well, she has published a best-selling book: *"How to Embrace Your Inner Hotness: An Inside Out Approach to a Lasting Makeover."*

A flannel-clad member of the setup crew for her dad's mobile-home-moving company, Leta Greene was raised in what she calls two extremes: truck stops and Provo, Utah. Not exactly spots that belched up beauty tips. So how did a shy tomboy with her share of scars become a confident beauty expert? Here's a clue: it didn't involve a traditional makeover, or even much makeup! She discovered the secret to *lasting* beauty—and it worked despite all the scars and truck stops.

Now she works tirelessly to share that secret, both as the founder of Glamour Connection®, a makeup and image consulting company, and as one of the most influential women of SeneGence International.

She speaks on more than just beauty, however: she talks about life in a way that makes you laugh your heart out! Leta has been featured on major local TV and radio stations as a beauty, self-image, and mind-set expert. What does this talented woman consider her most important accomplishment? "Easy!" she laughs. "My husband and children still like me!"

Leta has been through numerous trials in her life, many of which are detailed in her book and her speaking content. More than just a speaker on beauty and image, she speaks on life: how to deal with tragedy, change, and making commitments to one's self through goal setting that works! She also has mastered an amazing ability to stay positive and choose happiness despite life's trials and tragedies.

Leta Greene
Speaker, Author, Makeup Artist, Mom
leta@letagreene.com
letagreene.com
f https://www.facebook.com/Leta-Greene-aka-Hotness-
1569835053280205/?fref=ts

NATIONAL SPEAKERS ASSOCIATION

NSA®

MOUNTAIN WEST
Idaho, Montana, Utah, Wyoming

The Advice Collection Volume I

by Martin Hurlburt, the Money Whisperer
www.IfMoneyCouldTalk.com

WITHIN TEN MINUTES of coming into my office, the wife of a prominent doctor was in tears. She explained that she and her husband were on the verge of divorce. He had finished his medical training 10 years earlier with $500,000 in student loans. After a decade of earning hundreds of thousands of dollars a year, they were $1 million in debt. Somehow, they had managed to double what they owed! Financial stress was tearing them apart and she didn't know what to do.

I realized immediately that poor financial management was a symptom, but not the problem. Most advisors would put them on a strict budget and create a plan with lots of pretty graphs and spreadsheets. But I didn't think that would work. What would you do?

You'll get the rest of their story throughout this essay.

The purpose of almost everything I do is help people lead a happier, less stressful, and more productive life by getting their financial house in order. In this essay I will specifically help you understand the biggest challenge most of us face when it comes to managing money and how your financial choices impact your health, your relationships, and virtually every area of your life.

Let me start by saying I love money! But don't get me wrong. I'm not greedy. I live a modest lifestyle and drive modest cars. What I love about money is studying the behavioral side of it. Why do some people succeed and others never quite get the hang of it? One thing I can tell you for sure is that financial success has very little to do with your level of income or your level of education. I've worked with highly educated doctors, attorneys, and business executives who earn hundreds of thousands of dollars per year. And yet, they are a financial disaster when they walk into my office.

I've made it my life's mission to understand why that happens and how others can avoid similar mistakes. For 25 years I've read every book I could about behavioral economics, financial habits, and the psychology of money. I've written a few books, created training programs on developing better financial habits. and lectured extensively on the subject.

I can summarize the most important lesson I've learned in seven key words. When properly understood and applied, these seven key words can make almost anyone's situation better. You might be managing a multi-million dollar portfolio or struggling with debt. You might be earning $1 million a year or you might be a schoolteacher with a modest income. These seven words can help! Are you ready for them?

Emotions can be hazardous to your wealth!

Let me explain what I mean by that, how it impacts you and your family, as well as offer a simple solution that will take about 15 minutes to do. I'll also refer back to the doctor and his wife from time to time.

Eight out of 10 people list money as the biggest cause of stress in their lives today. That means it causes more stress than everything else combined! Marital and relationship problems, drug and alcohol abuse—all the other problems out there stacked up together cause less stress than managing your money.

There are many reasons why dealing with financial issues can cause so much stress. In my full training course, I reveal several of them. In this essay, I'll focus on just one and it's a biggie: information overload.

Your brain has two basic parts: a rational part that wants to carefully consider all options and choose the best one, and an emotional part that wants to avoid pain or get pleasure now. The emotional part also has a built in fight-or-flight instinct. Things go smoothly when these two parts work together.

For thousands of years, our species survived by using the emotional "avoid pain, get pleasure now" part of the brain. Our ancestors' whole focus was on how to get something to eat and provide or maintain some basic shelter. They also wanted to avoid the many real dangers that surrounded them almost constantly. Instincts and emotional reactions helped them survive. Is it any wonder then that the emotional side of our brain is so powerful?

Up until recently, the luxury of thinking rationally and planning things out was something that only kings and very rich people could afford. It has only been in the last century or two that the common person could provide for their basic needs and have some time left over to think. In terms of the history of mankind, we were given the gift of time just a short while ago. We have used that time to create great advances in technology, medicine, science, and an increase in our overall knowledge base.

While an increase in knowledge has many advantages, it also has some major disadvantages. One study showed that in 2011, Americans took in five times more information every day than they did in 1986. It comes in the form of emails, tweets, 300 channels on cable TV, YouTube, Facebook and more.

With an overwhelming amount of information and choices being thrust upon us, our brains are getting tired. Specifically, the left and logical side of our brain is getting worn-out. Literally.

An excellent clarification of this problem is described in *The Organized Brain* by Daniel J. Levitin:

> Neurons are living cells with a metabolism; they need oxygen and glucose to survive and when they've been working hard, we experience fatigue. Every status update you read on Facebook, every tweet or text message you get from a friend, is competing for resources in your brain with important things like whether to put your savings in stocks or bonds.

No wonder your brain is so fatigued! It is constantly being asked to process information and make decisions.

When your rational brain is tired from all of those choices, the emotional side is allowed to take over. This observation was discovered in a fascinating study at MIT. Students were divided into two groups and each one was asked to memorize some numbers. One group had to remember seven numbers and the other only two numbers. That was not the experiment. What happened next was.

When they were done, each group was asked if they would like something to eat and offered cake or fruit. One group overwhelmingly chose fruit and the other cake. Any guesses which was which?

In the group asked to memorize seven numbers, almost everyone chose cake. The other group preferred fresh fruit. Scientists concluded that the brains of those who remembered seven numbers were tired and when presented with cake or fruit, the emotional side took over and grabbed some delicious cake. Those who memorized two numbers were less fatigued and able to realize that fruit was a better choice.

Let's now put this newfound knowledge in the context of managing your money. Imagine this: after making literally thousands of small choices in a day and being inundated with information, it's 8pm and you need to figure out how to rollover that old 401k that's been ignored for too long. Your brain is tired.

You type "how to invest" into Google and it lists 267,000,000 websites! If you looked at 100 websites per day for 365 days a year, it would take you 73 years to get through them all. Even if you managed to do it, what would you accomplish? Absolutely nothing! And in the process, you might lose your family, your job, and everything that matters to you. One hundred websites a day with no vacations for 73 years would probably alienate those around you.

To make matters worse, many of the websites conflict. Then you have the Wall Street Journal, CNN Money, Fortune Magazine, Jim Kramer yelling at you on TV, and Fox Business News with those numbers scrolling across the bottom of your TV screen. With all of this conflicting information overloading your senses, you're supposed to make an intelligent decision with your money? Ha!

What do you usually do when you're faced with an important financial choice and you feel overwhelmed and confused? It's typically one of two things: make a decision or delay the decision. Let's look at each of these outcomes.

If you make a decision while your brain is tired and feeling overwhelmed, which side of your brain do you think is in charge? Is it the logical side or the emotional side? Chances are, it is the emotional side. You want to get it over with and end up doing whatever feels right in the moment.

This switch to the emotional explains why you sometimes make a choice and later regret it. Have you ever bought something or made an investment, and a year later wished you hadn't? As you look back, you say to yourself, "What was I thinking?" Chances are the rational side of your brain had been overworked and the emotional side took over. You literally were NOT thinking!

Or maybe you went with the second option of not deciding anything at all. Instead, you threw it in your financial junk drawer and delayed making that choice. All of us have kitchen junk drawers. They are filled with things that may or may not work, and we may not need them. We are not sure what to do, so we throw it in the junk drawer.

When I meet with a couple for the first time, their financial situation can often be best described as a financial junk drawer. All of these junk drawers follow a similar pattern. They are full of accounts and insurance plans that the couple is not sure what to do with. So in the drawer it goes, which allows them to delay making a decision.

Other things you may find in a financial junk drawer are old IRAs and 401Ks or maybe a savings bond your grandmother bought when you were five.

Postponing these important decisions does not make them go away, nor does it reduce your financial stress. It may offer a little bit of temporary relief, but over time, the problem builds up and gets worse.

Whether your financial stress comes from making emotional decisions you later regret or delaying decisions, or both, the stress adds up.

The cost of financial worry can be huge. And it goes far beyond dollars and cents, interest rates and debt. How can you measure the cost in human terms? What if the doctor and his wife get divorced? What does that cost them as a couple? What does it cost their children? The hospital where he works? Their community? When a family falls apart, the impact can be staggering.

One study showed that people with high levels of financial stress are:

- 2.5 times more likely to suffer from ulcers and stomach problems.

- 5 times more likely to suffer from depression.

- 10 times more likely to have headaches or migraines.

It's my belief that financial stress impacts virtually every area of your life. Your relationships, your health, and your emotional well-being are all impacted by how well you control your money. It's often said that money is a leading cause of divorce. That's partially true. It's not money that leads to divorce, but rather a lack of communication about money. The solution I'll offer at the end of this will go a long way in helping you improve the communication between you and your partner when you talk about finances.

So what is the solution? How can you eliminate or at least reduce the stress in your life when it comes to managing money?

A popular myth is that having more money will solve your financial problems. That's not true. Often more money makes matters worse. If money solved financial problems, then every lottery winner would live happily ever after. But the majority loses it. And some lose more than just the money. They lose family, friends, and even end up divorced.

In the case of the doctor and his wife, income and money were NOT the problem. They had plenty of it. So, if the answer to your financial problems is not having more money, what is it?

The answer is to make better choices.

People who succeed financially are not better looking or smarter than the rest of us. They don't work any harder or have special skills compared to others. They have simply learned how to make better decisions than the rest of us. And what drives all of our financial decisions? It's how we think our choices will make us feel. Hence the phrase, emotions can be hazardous to your wealth.

As it turned out, the doctor in my story dealt with the stress of practicing medicine with reckless spending. He was constantly buying things he didn't need. What he actually needed was a mental break from the pressure of patient care, paperwork, and everything else that goes into running a practice. He found that he could let go of all of that, temporarily, by going online and looking for things to buy. He loved doing the research and comparisons. He loved finding a good deal, even when it was something he didn't really want or need.

When I teach classes about how to develop better financial habits, I show a picture of the very first iPhone being sold in my hometown at one minute past midnight. People surrounding the buyer are literally applauding and have looks of joy on their faces. The caption below says, "This is pretty much the single best experience of my life!" Think about it. The single best experience of her life was spending $500 on a phone at one minute past midnight. What happened to the price of that phone two months later? It dropped by half. iPhone is currently on their 6th generation. The single best experience of her life is now obsolete.

Did she have to have that phone at one minute past midnight? No. Why did she do it? Because of how it made her feel. There are some people who get a thrill and true emotional satisfaction from having the latest and greatest technology.

Maybe that doesn't describe you, but you are not immune from the impact of emotions and how they influence your spending decisions. The car you drive, the kind of clothes you buy, where you go out to eat, and where you vacation. Virtually every spending decision you make is based on how you think it will make you feel. This logic applies to people on both ends of the spectrum: those who are frugal, those who are spend-a-holics, and everyone in-between.

Now let's look at emotions and investing. Many studies have shown that emotional responses to investment trends can lead to lower returns.

Fidelity conducted a study on the performance of its flagship Magellan mutual fund during the tenure of its famous manager Peter Lynch. He ran the Fidelity Magellan fund from 1977-1990, delivering an astonishing 29% average annual return. Despite his remarkable performance while running the fund, Fidelity found that the average investor actually lost money during his 13-year tenure. How is that possible? According to Fidelity, investors would run for the doors during periods of poor performance and come rushing in after periods of success. Such behavior, commonly known as performance chasing, is something that affects the great majority of investors and is one of the reasons that most investors never experience the returns they expect.

When it comes to managing your spending, your investments and everything to do with money, I hope that you'll agree that emotions can be hazardous to your wealth. They drive your financial decisions and can add stress to your lives that impacts your health, your relationships, your spirituality, and your overall happiness and well-being. So what can you do about it?

Discover and understand your money personality.

Imagine that you're driving on the freeway at 75 mph. It's a speed at which you feel comfortable. Suddenly, someone whizzes by you at 90 mph. What do you think of that person? Do you praise their driving skills and ability to go fast? No! You probably think they are a danger on the streets and ought to lose their license. While you are in the middle of that thought, you come up behind someone who is driving 10 mph slower than you and you can't get around them. What do you think of that person? Do you praise their cautious nature? No! You probably think they are a danger on the streets and ought to lose their license.

You tend to drive at a speed that is comfortable for you, and you think that anyone who drives faster or slower than you is dangerous.

The same thinking applies to the way you manage your money. You try to do it in a way that feels comfortable to you. You can't understand anyone who takes more or less risk than you. You can't understand someone who saves, spends, or invests differently than you. And chances are you are married to that person. This is what leads to conflicts in a marriage and not the money itself.

There are five basic money personalities:

1. Spender.

2. Saver.

3. Risk-taker.

4. Conservative.

5. Flyer.

One personality is not better than another. You should not try to change yours or that of your spouse. It's better to recognize, understand, and respect each one.

In a related example, if a risk-taker comes into my office and I create for them a conservative strategy, they probably won't stick with it, even if the plan is likely to achieve their goals and do so with minimum risk. They get a sense of emotional satisfaction from taking risk.

A primary function of any good wealth manager is not to tell their clients what to feel or how much risk to take. It's not good to recommend to each person the same thing they recommend to everyone else, even if it's a great idea. A good wealth manager should try to understand how his or her client really feels about money and then build a plan around it.

You will begin to make better choices with your money and reduce your stress levels when you embrace your personality rather than ignore it or try to override it. It's very easy to get caught up in current trends and what's popular now. You may feel some pressure to join the crowd, even if doing so goes against your personality. Don't do it!

It's simple to find out what your money personality is. Go to www.IfMoney-CouldTalk.com. You will find a link on the home page. Click on it and answer some questions. For each one, choose the answer that first pops into your head without overthinking.

You'll get a special report within two business days. It will outline the strengths and weaknesses of each personality profile, including yours. The report will also give you ideas on how to better manage your money and still be who you are.

Going back to the example of my doctor client, here's how he'd fare with mainstream financial advice. Most financial professionals who don't deal with or understand money personalities would put him on a strict budget and cut off any unnecessary spending until he built up his savings. That won't work. While it's technically right, it doesn't take into consideration his profile. If his plan is not adjusted to meet his money personality, he won't stick with it.

Instead, I told him to set a goal of saving $2,000 a month. His reward would be to spend $200 of it, netting him $1,800. Spenders get a sense of relief whether the dollar amount is $20 or $20,000. He just needed the release that came with looking for and buying things online. I didn't want to take that away from him completely. This is a plan that is more likely to get results because it is sustainable.

Remember near the start of this essay I said money doesn't cause divorce but rather it's a lack of communication about money. You and your spouse should each find out what your money personality is. It's important to do this separately so that you do not influence each other's answers. You'll be surprised at the insights this simple exercise gives you.

Imagine that a couple is driving across country. The husband wants to drive 12 hours a day and get there as soon as possible. His wife likes to stop at places of interest along the way and enjoy the journey. Do you think that might cause some conflict along the way? Who is right?

Neither one is right or wrong. They are just different. If they each understand and respect how the other feels, they will have a much more peaceful journey than if they each try to prove that their way is right. An example of the compromise would look like this: Instead of three 12-hour days of driving, the husband might agree to five days of just over seven hours each. And instead of wanting to stop at every historic marker along the way, the wife might agree to plan in advance and pick just one or two places of interest each day.

If you would like to get on the road to leading a happier, less stressful, and more productive life, the first step on your journey is to discover your money personality. Go to www.IfMoneyCouldTalk.com.

It's Your Money. It's Your Future. TAKE CHARGE!

The information, tools and services presented in this document are provided to you for informational purposes only and are not to be used or considered as an offer of the solicitation of any offer to sell or to buy or subscribe for securities or other financial instruments. The information contained herein has been derived from sources believed to be reliable but is not guaranteed as to accuracy. Investors should consider this information as only a single factor in making their investment decision. Action taken by an investor should be based on their personal investment objectives and risk tolerance. Further information on

About the Author

Martin Hurlburt and other experts have put together this collection of their best material. Each essay stays focused on one point without adding any fluff. It's like having 15 condensed books in one. They are designed to uplift, teach and inspire.

Why should you read it? In real life, love, leadership, money and success are interwoven. A great leader truly cares for others. How well we manage our money impacts our family and those who matter most to us. *And in the end, success is really about combining your love for others, your leadership talent and your money (and other resources) in a focused effort to create good in the world.*

Those who manage to do this will achieve a sense of peace and happiness that cannot be had in any other way.

If that is important to you, then read this book!

Martin Hurlburt has a simple mission… To change the way people view themselves, their money and the impact money has on their lives. He understands that how well someone controls their money can, and will, impact their health, their relationships, the quality of their work and yes, even their happiness. However, his message goes beyond just money. It is about getting past the financial issues that plague so many of us and focusing on the more important things in life. To learn more, visit www.IfMoneyCouldTalk.com.

Martin Hurlburt

The Money Whisperer

512 W 300 North

801-477-0444

Martin@TM-Wealth.com

www.IfMoneyCouldTalk.com

ifmoneycouldtalk

NATIONAL SPEAKERS ASSOCIATION

NSA®

MOUNTAIN WEST
Idaho, Montana, Utah, Wyoming

Love Yourself Enough to Fail

by Michelle McCullough

THIS YEAR I have been learning an expensive and emotionally wrenching truth: Regret feels worse than failure.

If I could go back to my younger self, I would tell her, "Don't be afraid to fail. Fail faster! Failing can teach you amazing things."

Back in college I worked at an advertising agency in beautiful St. George, Utah. The agency was in the center of town and I moved to an apartment that was about a mile away. One day I decided I was going to rollerblade to work.

Let me pause this story for one minute to say this: Michelle McCullough is a sedentary lass. My idea of an Olympic sport is from the couch to the kitchen. I'm attempting to reform in my older years. I exercise 3-5 times a week and I've even run a half-marathon in my day. But the fact that I wanted to get on rollerblades and roll to work back then was completely out of my athletic comfort zone. That said, Michelle McCullough is also a daring and committed lass, and sometimes I like to do hard things just to do them.

So…I set off on my roommate's rollerblades in my business clothes, with my shoes in a backpack. Can you picture it? This was my third or fourth time ever rollerblading. I was an avid roller skater in my elementary school days—and I was mighty good at the backwards skate, I might add—but the back stoppy things on the rollerblades never made sense to me or I was just too uncoordinated to figure it out. I had my own roller blade braking system, simply rolling onto the grass.

My stroll to the business park was uneventful and just as I was feeling like I could conquer the world, I entered the business park from the rear entrance. What I never realized in a vehicle is that the parking lot has an ever so slight decline, and as I start to gain speed, I saw no grass.

Cue the dramatic music. To get to my business building, I have to roll around the complex to the front of the block. I turn the first corner at a dangerous speed, and while still processing my decisions, I see an old school—think London style—phone booth in the corner. Just as athletic ability was not my strong suit, I didn't excel in physics either. My naive brain said, "Just roll up to

that phone booth. You'll tap it with your hands and bring your body to a stop."
My sheer speed had me crash full body into the phone booth and I promptly fell
backwards onto the pavement. It knocked the wind—and the humility—out of
me. I just stayed on the ground for a few minutes catching my breath and waiting for the cars that witnessed this great event to pass by.

I took off the rollerblades and walked the final distance into my office.

Rollerblading was an utter, embarrassing failure.

I could have taken this experience as a testament to my lack of physical
ability and never try anything like this again. Or I could look at it with my experienced eyes and ask myself the questions, "What worked? What didn't? What
needs to change?"

These three questions are my favorite for evaluating ANY failure. When we
look at my graceful attempt at rollerblading, what worked?

Well, I did some physical activity instead of taking the car to work. I got some
fresh air and some exercise. I realized that I needed more training and practice
and that I should probably learn how to use the back breaks.

What didn't work? Me + roller blades. And, let's be honest, my khaki overalls
and business shirt were the wrong "tool for the job."

What needs to change? I can still exercise on my way to work, and leave the
car at home, but I can walk or run in more appropriate attire and change at the
office.

Simple.

I wish I could say this was my only "failure." The truth is, I've had a lot of
them in every aspect of my life. I'm a "Make It Happen" kind of girl. I wrote a
book, created a radio show, started a video series and I've spoken to thousands
of people, essentially created a whole brand around those three words. But it
turns out that determination does not always equal immediate results.

I love entrepreneurship. I've started, sold, grown, and, if I'm being honest,
killed lots of businesses. But those businesses taught me A LOT and they make
my current businesses thrive.

I've said the wrong thing at the wrong time in an important relationship.
But I've learned how to be better at communicating and to get my point across
in a way that tries not to offend. And I've learned that I'm not weak if I need to
say, "I'm sorry."

I've dropped weights on my feet, eaten a bug that flew in my mouth on a
run, and I've sprayed myself with a can of mace (all true stories), but I've learned
ways that I can exercise without injuring myself.

I've spent money on multiple marketing outlets. And yet, when I've asked
myself these three powerful questions I can start to evaluate my messages better.

I critically look at mediums I choose and I scrutinize my target market to ensure that I'm hitting the correct audience.

Here's another great example of my evaluation questions "at work": As a marketing and advertising enthusiast, I loved when social media came onto the playing field. It gave me fun to ways to connect with old friends and it also gave me new outlets to promote my clients. But when things were REALLY new, I didn't like that some companies were "hitting the jackpot" while others were "just bobbing along." I didn't like the answer that some companies were "just lucky," so I set out to create a simple, yet effective social media plan for business-es. I used my own business's social media accounts as test cases. I tried different amounts of tweets and posts, different lengths and links, different times of day and different types of content.

Some weeks we saw great returns on our engagement, followers, traffic to our website, and greater conversion on our events and sales. Some weeks we just flat-lined. But every week, success or failure, I asked myself those three questions and refined my tests. I was also really conscious of the fact that most of my clients were small businesses and even solo entrepreneurs. Without a big budget or big team, they couldn't afford to spend all day online and still get the rest of their work done. I was determined to find a routine that didn't take eight hours a day. And after a few years (yes, YEARS) of trial and error, and evaluating every failure for greater results, I created what I now call "The Social Media Blueprint for Busi-ness." I help experts, authors, speakers and business owners learn how to utilize social media in just 15 minutes a day. Sure, there are other programs and systems out there, but this one is tried and true for my own businesses and clients.

Those questions refined me and made my system better and they work in every aspect of life. When I look at the categories used in Ann Webb's Ideal Life-Vision, they encompass every aspect of life into five areas: personal, profession-al, health, relationships, and spiritual. Just asking those questions every week for each of these life areas has changed my life and taught me ways to always be progressing. I can look at "What needs to change?" and move things around on my to do list, lighten a busy schedule, or reach out for help where appropriate. Simple weekly evaluation helps me create intentional weeks and I'm more effec-tive and productive.

That said, even great plans can hit stumbling blocks. But we have to stop looking at those experiences as "signs we shouldn't proceed" and start looking at them for what they truly are. I call them "trials of our fate"—simple challeng-es that really hit the core of our convictions to test if we really want the results we desire. They happen to everyone. It's the strong and the brave who power through that get results.

Even though I've figured out how to dissect my failures to turn them into great learning and improving experiences, sometimes I resist new opportunities out of fear. I've delayed book deals, relationships, employee compliments, meaningful conversations with my husband—all because I was too scared of the outcome. In the end, I missed big paychecks, opportunities to improve relationships because the timing changed, and opportunities to boost the self-esteem of others because I censored myself. This year specifically I lost speaking engagements, coaching clients, and promotional deals with major media because I was scared about putting myself out there. I was worried I was not healthy enough, too inexperienced, or that people would think I was just plain lame. I didn't try because I didn't want to fail. And I learned one of the most important lessons in my life: regret feels worse than failure.

I remember lots of regrets, even dating back to my single digits. I regret not keeping in touch with Alicia Gabica and Crystal Wilcox from Morningside Elementary in Twin Falls, Idaho. To this day, I still think about them.

I regret not having more conversations with my father. There were times when I said, "Oh dad, let me _____ (watch a movie, talk with my friends, go out with my friends) instead of making me sit here with you having a dumb conversation." My dad's conversations were deep and meaningful and by the time I could fully appreciate them, he passed away in his 50s.

I regret proposals I didn't submit, deadlines I missed and I always wonder, "What would have happened if I didn't let my fear get in the way and I actually did it?" I'll never know. I could have still failed, but I would have been no worse off than when I started. But if I had succeeded, how great that would have been!

I regret opportunities I was handed to share uplifting messages and simple compliments with strangers and loved ones. I still remember those opportunities and wish I could change them.

At least if I fail, I can say that I tried. At least if I fail, I can say that I learned a way NOT to do something.

I love the oft-quoted, "I have not failed. I have just found 10,000 ways that won't work," from Thomas Edison. If he had given up and not persisted through the trial of his fate, it would have changed our lives significantly.

What do you need to try 9,999 more times so you can succeed?

I don't want that to sound overwhelming, but I want to start thinking about our failures in a new way. Instead of fearing them, we need to embrace them and jump on the opportunity to learn.

The good news is we can also learn from other people's failures. One of my favorite principles in Jack Canfield's book The Success Principles is "Success Leaves Clues." The truth is, failure does, too.

Pastor Steve Furtick wisely stated, "One of the reasons we struggle with insecurity is that we compare our 'behind the scenes' to other people's highlight reel." Though some people are more public than others about their trials, everyone is having them. The world needs peak performers like you to set the example of how to accept failures, dust off, and move on with your head held high. Whether you face a business failure, a divorce, a missed opportunity, a lost sale, a fumbled business presentation—or all of the above—own it, learn from it, and envision a successful future and then go Make It Happen.

The Plastic Bag Principle

I was only seven at the time, but the memory of that night is still clear as ever.

It was past my bedtime. I was playing in my room, trying to go undetected, and thinking I was somehow cheating the system. When my mom finally came into my room, she handed me a plastic grocery sack and told me, "Pack some clothes. We're going to Grandma's house and I don't know when we're coming back."

I can't recall if I asked a lot of questions, but I distinctly remember putting a few items of clothing in my bag, and then adding some of my seven-year-old treasures—toys and all the coins to my name—which was probably less than fifty cents. The heavier items sank to the bottom of the bag and pulled it downward. I carefully carried it as we walked past my dad, who sat crying on the stairs. In my mind I can still see his figure illuminated through the window as we drove away in the dark.

Isn't it interesting the things we remember, and the things we forget, years later? I've never looked at that event as being overly traumatic, and it has never caused the need for any professional counseling sessions. However, the experience has given me a good mental image for the baggage we all carry.

I bet if you and I were to sit down, you could tell me some crazy and maybe even downright depressing situations you've encountered in your life. If we invited a few neighbors or friends, there's no doubt they could each tell us stories that would make us cringe or cry.

Each of us has baggage in some form or another. Some is more public than others. Some is more tragic than others. But no matter what, we all have something. Divorce, abuse, loss of a loved one, loss of a job, severe economic consequences, significant health issues, caring for an ailing spouse or parent, caring for a child with disabilities—the list goes on and on.

It's easy to get caught up comparing hardships and trying to outdo one another in a "my life is worse than yours" kind of competition. At times I have to remind myself of the old saying, "If we hung our problems on the line, you'd take yours, and I'd take mine." Life is hard in its own way for each of us, but it's not your past or circumstances that define you.

When my mother handed me that grocery sack, I could have asked her a lot of questions. I could have requested a nicer bag. After all, my grandfather was a travel agent and we had Pan AM overnight bags in abundance in our house. But what difference would it have made? We can package our trials however we want, but they still remain the same. They are still trials, and we can choose to dwell on them or deal with them. We can look at them as something temporary we will carry with us for a time before leaving them behind, or we can make them a permanent fixture in our lives that we lug with us into every relationship, employment opportunity, and circumstance.

Don't spend your whole life wishing your "bag" was different. You have to use what you've got, learn from the experiences, and move on to create a better future.

Again, I know many people will say, "Your parents got divorced when you were seven? That isn't nearly as traumatic as _____." I get it. I could tell you some of my other life events and hardships to try and convince you I've been through trials, but the same principle would apply. It's not a competition, it's life. But please, please, please, don't let your bag become your identity.

I was at a live event when I first heard the story of Sam Bracken. His childhood was fraught with trial and drama. He was abused by his stepfather and started using drugs and alcohol by the age of nine. He struggled through school, but with the help of caring teachers and his involvement in sports, he was able to turn his life around. Then, just as things were looking up, his mother abandoned him when he was fifteen, and he was left homeless with only the clothes on his back and a few other possessions in an orange sports duffle bag.

As I listened to Bracken—who later became a scholar, star athlete, and successful business executive—share his story, I was moved. Then he taught a powerful life principle. He said, "Fill your bag with hopes and dreams instead of fears and insecurities."

Dwelling on what's not right will never bring you the success and happiness you desire. Choosing success despite your challenges will give you power and purpose beyond measure. However, if you've spent most of your life dwelling in the past or wallowing in self-pity, it may take a while to re-train your brain (and even your relationships) to a point that you're willing to make that kind of shift. Remember, it takes practice. If you're finding it hard to simply move on, you may want to consider seeking professional help to get you on your way.

One of the most powerful practices of peak performers is to overcome the past and become something better. They don't let their circumstances, past or current, keep them from high achievement. They acknowledge the experiences for what they are: stepping stones. You have that choice, too. Each trial in your life is designed to teach you something and move you further down the path of progression. When you look at them from that standpoint, you can face and overcome them in powerful ways.

Whether you're seven or seventy-seven, it's not too late to accept what's in your bag and make the most of it. The principles and practices in this book are designed to help you do just that, so as a final note in practicing failure, I encourage you to embrace your past and present failures so you can create a new and experienced future.

Some of us are holding on to past failures like baggage. Those failures enter the home, the work place, every relationship, and every conversation. This is a mistake that has an expensive ripple effect.

What I want for you, for my kids, for my friends, and for strangers on the street is to let our failures teach us instead of weighing us down. I want us to recognize those failures as teachers and not brick walls.

As I mentioned before I'm learning the expensive lesson "regret feels worse than failure." My failures hold me back and cost me money. It's because I'm looking at them as labels and baggage. It's time to look at them as steps and stages that are here to help us be better, to elevate us.

Take some time to reframe your past so it can stop holding you back. Give yourself permission to keep failing so you can learn. I'm not saying we should do things unprepared or sloppy. It's okay to plan and try to avoid mistakes, but don't use failure as an excuse.

You can make excuses or you can MAKE IT HAPPEN.

About the Author

When many 12-year-olds were asking for Sony Walkmans and Girbaud jeans, Michelle McCullough was begging her mom for a Franklin Day Planner. She was elated on Christmas morning to open a box of success goodness and spent that holiday break writing a mission statement, prioritizing to-do lists, and getting organized. Today, more than twenty years later, Michelle's expertise in motivation and marketing appears online, on television, radio and print. She helps entrepreneurs and professionals master productivity, time management, leadership, and peak performance.

Michelle took advantage of her early success and business education and started her first business, Doodads Promotional Products, when she was nineteen. Doodads has run "in the black" every year since its inception. Michelle has also created, grown and/or sold four additional businesses in the last fifteen years. Her successful experiences created a demand for her business consulting skills, and she has spent ten years coaching and consulting with small business owners worldwide.

Michelle is a sought-after professional speaker and trainer, teaching business and success principles to corporations and associations. Whether it's a group of high powered entrepreneurs or a room full of high-energy youth, Michelle captivates, motivates and inspires.

Michelle's been seen on HP's Small Business website, on Entrepreneur.com, and in Utah Business Magazine. She's worked with top brands like Visa Small Business, UPS Store, AWeber and more. She's been interviewed on numerous radio and television shows, and she was named one of the "40 under 40". Additionally, Michelle is the managing director of Startup Princess, an international organization for women entrepreneurs where they have over 300,000 followers on twitter and were named by Forbes as one of the top ten resources for women entrepreneurs.

Michelle is also the best-selling author of "The Time Blueprint for Entrepreneurs" and "The Make It Happen Blueprint". She's the creator of "The Social Media Blueprint", "The Life Balance Myth" and "Marketing Mastery" consulting programs. You can find her regularly on the air on Make It Happen Radio & The Living Room Radio. Whether on the air or on the stage Michelle loves to share her top tips in motivation and marketing for peak performers. With two kids and still a planner in tow, Michelle knows there's no time to mess around, it's time to Make It Happen!

Michelle McCullough
Best-Selling Author & Speaker
www.speakmichelle.com
facebook.com/speakmichelle
twitter.com/speakmichelle
instagram.com/speakmichelle
Make It Happen!

MICHELLE M^CCULLOUGH

Speaker • • Success Coach • • Show Host

The Power of Love

NWA 255 CRASH

by Mitch Seehusen

IT WAS A warm, muggy summer evening. The kind that soaked my shirt in perspiration and made it stick to the small of my back. The setting sun glowed an eerie orange.

I had just landed at Detroit Metro Airport in Romulus, Michigan.

I collected my bags and headed to the long-term parking structure. My company van was parked on the top-level parking deck, facing west. I opened the back of the van, placed my suit bag and briefcase inside and closed the door.

Then I heard it, the revving of the commercial jet engines. I quickly spun around. In front of me was a Northwest Airlines MD82 engines at full power, brakes applied and then, released and rolling north up the main runway. I watched, transfixed on the scene. The plane raced down the runway. To the horizon, I watched and waited for the familiar site of the nose of the plane then the fuselage, wings and tail lifting skyward.

But, it did not happen. Suddenly there was a huge plume cloud of smoke and fire past the end of the runway. A much larger fiery, billowing black and grey mushroom cloud of smoke and fire followed. My heart sank, fearing the worst. I quickly opened the driver's door of the van. Key in the ignition, turn, hurry, hurry, hurry. From park to drive in an instant. The Aerostar leapt forward, then down the winding ramp, around, around and around again. Finally to the pay booth, credit card, receipt. Then out. Towards the airport exit and the I-94 freeway. My destination was to the left, west to freedom, my hotel, my assignment, dinner, sleep. But, I was drawn right, to the east, towards Detroit, towards tragedy.

I drove the 4.7 miles quickly, faster than the First Responders. I came upon the wreckage, fire and tragedy of the crash. I stopped on the right shoulder of the freeway bridge over Middlebelt road and rolled down the passenger window. I parked on the freeway bridge that crossed Middlebelt road and I wept, overcome with emotion, sadness, for all of those who had just perished in an instant.

The wreckage was horrendous. Middlebelt road was all on fire. An endless tower of flames now lit up the night sky, as well as both sides of the hillsides on either side for as far as I could see to the south. Darkness had come, but the burning jet fuel lit up the night sky. The acrid smell burned my nose and throat. My eyes watered and I was certain that I would vomit.

The sounds of the sirens of first responders drew closer. I slipped the van once again into drive rolling the vehicle east, away from the crash, away from this horrendous scene. A couple of exits further east on I-94, I exited the freeway. At a stoplight it occurred to me that I needed to turn around. I made my way on city streets and small highways to the west and towards Jackson, Michigan. My final destination for that night, like so many Sunday nights before, towards safety, quiet, comfort and hopefully sleep.

I arrived at the Holiday Inn with its trademark Holidome. No stop for food or a dip in the swimming pool. I quickly checked in, key in hand, found my room and immediately turned on the television. Special reports interrupted regular programming about a plane crash at Detroit Metro Airport. Details to follow on the 11 o'clock news. I waited impatiently for 11 o'clock to arrive.

The local news reported very little detailed information. After all it was a plane crash at night in the dark. It was a Northwest Airlines Jet headed for Orange County California, John Wayne Airport. Everyone on board was presumed dead. They were not certain if anyone had been killed on the ground. It was not until the next morning that we would learn that a miracle had occurred amidst so much tragedy.

An Arizona family had been on the flight returning home, a mother, father, son, and daughter. Cichan, who was dubbed the Miracle Child, was hospitalized for a fractured skull, broken leg, broken collarbone and third-degree burns over 30 percent of her body. Her parents and 6-year-old brother died in the crash. Cichan lived with an aunt, uncle and cousin in Birmingham, Ala., after the crash. She was hospitalized in the burn unit at the University of Michigan hospital for nearly two months until October 9th, 1987.

Little Cecelia Cichan had somehow survived the crash in the arms of her mother. Shielded from the fire and terrible destruction of the crash. She was found by a firefighter as he worked at the crash site. He heard whimpering and crying as he sifted through the charred wreckage of the plane. As he moved debris and turned it over there he discovered this sweet, small little girl. She had been shielded from the tumbling crash that ripped the plane apart by her mother. The debris field as you can imagine, stretched for several miles. And yet this small fragile child was saved by the loving embrace of her mother.

The ensuing fire that followed was all-consuming. A jet airliner loaded for a cross-country flight is really a large gasoline tank. Airline fuel is the most efficient. Kerosene actually, airplane grade is the purest of petroleum fuels. It has the lowest flash point, at lowest temperatures, it burns the hottest, the quickest and with the most energy from its combustion. That is one of the reasons that airline disasters are so tragic and quick. The crash at several hundred miles per hour is severe blunt force trauma. The fire upon impact or flashpoint is horrific. Thankfully it burns very fast and very hot. Little Cecelia's mother shielded her daughter from the rapidly moving intensely burning fire. It was her last living act of love. It truly was a miracle due to the power of her mother's love. The one organ that can never be measured by science or religion is the size and power of the human heart.

A Michigan miracle had somehow occurred. Through all of the anguish and pain of such monumental loss of life was somehow tempered by this sweet, small precious miracle child named Cecelia Cichan. She was at the University of Michigan hospital in the Intensive Care Burn Unit. There was little hope for her survival the morning after the crash.

The days that followed witnessing this crash were difficult for me. As Friday approached I would have been planning my return to the airport to fly home again to Salt Lake City for the weekend. We had other plans, as my wife Linda was flying out on Friday to Detroit to spend the weekend with me. This would save me the normal weekend trip and give her a chance to see my workplace, meet my work colleagues, and get a break from the grind of being a fifth grade teacher. It was her first break in the new school year teaching at a year- round school.

I had mixed emotions as that day approached. Of course she had heard about the crash. It was the top story on even the national news for a few days as 156 passengers and crew had perished in an instant.

I reassured her that "airline travel is still safer than driving in a car," which it continues to be to this day. Friday came and she arrived in Detroit. I picked her up in the same Ford Aerostar van. We had an enjoyable weekend together. We drove across the Ambassador International Bridge to Windsor, Ontario and were stopped at the customs station in Canada. Agents searched the entire van including the contents of my golf bag in the back. They treated us like common criminals. We had a company picnic on Saturday with my co-workers and had a relaxing time.

Sunday came and it was time for her to fly home. It was much easier and not much thought was given to that plane flight as there had been just a few days earlier. She made it home safely without incident and that was that. When Tuesday morning rolled around I was back at Detroit Metro to fly on TWA Airlines through St. Louis Missouri to Springfield, Missouri to visit our hose manufacturing plants in Northern Arkansas.

Terror gripped me as I sat in the window seat of the McDonnell Douglas MD82, the same model and manufacturer of plane that had just crashed a few nights earlier. It was still much too early for the NTSB to even speculate as to the cause of the crash. My stomach sank and turned over as we backed away from the gate and disconnected from the tug. The engines revved to life and the smell of jet fuel exhaust filled my nose, my senses and my mind with images, sounds and smells of that horrific scene just nine nights earlier. That first flight after witnessing such death and destruction was much harder than I had imagined. I was instantly transported back to that night to the exact location in my mind, reliving the event again.

My trip progressed without incident. That flight and the ones that followed proceeded without incident. As each trip progressed and time passed the memory of that night softened a bit. I did however, my research on the type of aircraft that would be serving me as I travelled from that point forward. The DC-9 MD82 aircraft was very popular with airlines as they were much more fuel-efficient than their Boeing 727 and 737 counterparts. But, what made them more fuel-efficient also made them more dangerous as they operated with 40% less horsepower. Less horsepower, less lift, less margin for error should another chain of events occur as happened with flight NWA255.

The NTSB came in and began the arduous task of inspecting the wreckage and attempting to learn the cause of the crash. The flight recorders were recovered and there were photos and video of the aftermath of the flight. At first it was believed to be pilot error. Initial findings determined that the front and rear wing flaps had not been set before takeoff. No front or back flaps meant less wing surface area, less lift and a much longer runway needed to get the proper lift to get airborne.

As time passed it was finally determined that it was a combination equipment failures, procedure and protocol missteps and pilot error that all contributed to the crash. The flight had been running behind schedule that day. NWA255 had originated that morning in Grand Rapids, Michigan and Phoenix was the flights final destination. Stopping in Orange County at night meant they had to honor noise abatement ordinances when they took off from John Wayne airport on their way to Phoenix. The later they departed on a Sunday night the more stringent the penalty. This would have required them to take off and immediately reduce power to the engines to quiet them just enough to avoid fines, which was another reason for their hurry and sense of getting back on schedule.

How could this disaster have actually happened? After all there should have been a very loud warning siren and audible alarm when flaps were not set before takeoff on a DC9 MD82 but there was not. After examining the flight recordings and the airplane wreckage, it was determined that the circuit breaker that provided power to this warning device may have popped out of its normal location on one end, breaking the electrical circuit and the alarm never sounded despite the flaps not being set.

As a result the plane ran down the runway to the north. It was unable to get the proper lift or altitude. The left wing tip clipped a light pole in the car rental parking lot. Twisting the plane and flipping it sharply to the right, and then dropping suddenly towards a railroad bridge that crossed middlebelt road. The right wing hit the bridge hard, rupturing the fuel tank and sent the plane cartwheeling up Middlebelt road as it burst into flames and ripped apart into millions of pieces.

Often times when something bad happens in our world there are a number of events that must all occur in succession or simultaneously for the "Perfect Storm" to occur. Working with very technical people on a daily basis I am often asked what went wrong? Why did this happen? What is the root cause of this failure?

Committees for this sort of thing are formed across many departments in the company. Representatives from purchasing, facilities, design engineering, manufacturing engineering and of course safety. We examine the problem or failure in minute detail. Meetings are held in person and virtually. Sometimes hundreds or even thousands of phone calls, faxes and e-mails are sent to make certain the "Event" is dissected and as many facets of the problem are identified. And still, after days, months and sometimes years of study one root cause is seldom determined. It is usually like inserting a key into a very complex lock. All of the tumblers must line up and turn in the appropriate order for the lock to open, or release.

As a result of these incidents some companies may change their direction. They may have something so terrible happen that the physical and emotional outcomes for those involved in the incident never really recover. Faulty and flawed decisions are made by these people and their companies struggle, merge, are sold and sometimes close.

A few years ago I came the realization that when I select my seat on an airplane especially on those with open seating, I usually sit right behind the wing, on the right side where I can see that the flaps are set before we taxi and take off. I have preferred to fly Boeing aircraft whenever possible. But I realized that after a few years these habits were not necessarily a conscious choice but rather an automatic decision based on years of habits following this life experience.

Over the next decade from that fateful night, with every business trip to Detroit I would notice the makeshift memorials that were placed on the hilltop above Middlebelt road. I was struck by how many wreaths, crosses, bouquets of flowers and plush toys were placed on the hilltop above the crash site. Many of the families of the passengers and crew members that perished that fateful night received no body to bury. Something that does not occur to you at first thought, is no body, no closure. It was a number of years until a permanent memorial was constructed and placed near the airport, a place for friends and family of those who lost a loved one in the crash to visit and grieve.

In February of 2011, I was able to gain more closure as an eye witness to this tragedy. While on a business trip I stopped on the side of the road near the permanent memorial and, climbed the hill into the grove of Austrian pines that surround the granite tribute to those who lost their lives on that August night. If you have ever flown into Detroit and rented a car, chances are you have driven on that very same road the NWA255 crashed upon.

As a result of Cecelia Chehan's young age, the seriousness of her injuries and losing both of her parents and brother in the same accident she lived a very private and protected life in Alabama with her aunt, uncle, and cousin.

It was 26 years after the accident before Cecelia spoke out in the media regarding the fateful accident August 16, 1987. She was a part of a documentary film chronicling the experiences of fourteen sole survivors of airplane crashes. Her account was surprisingly positive and optimistic despite losing her mother, father and brother at the same time.

In everyday life there are incidents of trauma that can force you to reevaluate your priorities. You may witness a fatal car crash or a terrible industrial or construction accident. That feeling of upset washes over you and caution becomes the prime motivator. You may drive a bit slower, pause a bit longer at a stop sign, or really look both ways several times to make certain no traffic is coming. Then as the days pass by that feeling of caution and pause give way to thoughts of the day. "Wow I really need to get to work." I wonder what my boss will say today that will really tick me off? I wonder what to have for dinner tonight? And ultimately, what will happen next on my favorite Television program or will my favorite sports team win tonight. As the days pass the feeling fades and the thoughts subside. The automatic process of the daily grind takes over and replaces that caution and concern.

As I grow older I realize that those of us who have experienced traumatic events and have found a way to make something positive out of the experience that we are merchants of hope in the work that we do. It does not matter our vocation or our avocation but all we really need is to focus on spreading a message of gratitude for our life's experience and hope for the future. The past is gone. Tomorrow is really only a hope. Today is the present. The only gift that we have to really make a difference and positively impact the lives of others is to be that person. Be that change. Be that Hope.

About the Author

Growing up in the great potato state of Idaho Mitch held a great number of odd jobs before settling on a career in Sales. From Business Owner to Traffic Safety Engineer, Mitch has tried many careers across several continents.

After graduating from Utah State University with a Bachelors Degree of Science, Mitch has yet to work as a Scientist. He does however own several lab coats. His ability to speak on almost any topic for as long as possible, lead to free college tuition and books.

Mitch and his family reside in the sleepy Salt Lake City suburb of South Jordan, Utah. He enjoys traveling throughout the country and world sharing his message of Safety, Love and Hope. Mitch currently serves as the President of the National Speakers Association Mountainwest Chapter.

Mitch Seehusen
Speaker, Futurist, Humorist
Lightspeed Networking
PO Box 95265, South Jordan, UT 84095
8018858892
speaker@mitchseehusen.com
www.mitchseehusen.com
facebook.com/mitchelseehusen
@mitchseehusen

Mitch Seehusen

The Love Choice

by Paul H. Jenkins, Ph.D.

VIKTOR FRANKL ENDURED one of the most disturbing chapters in our history books. He then rewrote that chapter as one of the most influential books of our time, *Man's Search for Meaning*.

Dr. Frankl was an Austrian psychiatrist who, because of his Jewish heritage, was arrested and imprisoned at Auschwitz by the Nazis. He was separated from his beloved wife and family, who were eventually murdered by their captors.

Viktor Frankl postulated, and his victorious life proved, that everything could be taken from us except "the last of the human freedoms – to choose one's attitude in any given set of circumstances..." This profound doctrine that one could choose a response, regardless of how things appear, was born and bred in the black hell of corruption, horror and atrocity known as Auschwitz.

Immaculée Ilibagiza crouched beside seven other women in a cramped twelve square foot bathroom in Rwanda for three months. They were careful not to make a sound so bloodthirsty Hutu killing raiders would not discover them and thrust their bodies onto the piles of rotting corpses that were Immaculée's family and fellow Tutsis.

To the accompaniment of screams and stench of death through the tiny bathroom window, Immaculée searched for and found love. Completely justified to hate the Hutus, Immaculée knew hate would only perpetuate and prolong decades of hatred, which caused the most devastating genocide of our time.

With the saintly dignity and poise of a modern-day Mother Teresa, Immaculée shares a powerful message of love and forgiveness with audiences around the world who have far less reason to hate.

Both Dr. Frankl and Immaculée knew they could not control their enemies' actions towards them, but they could choose and control their own attitude toward their enemies.

They did not choose their prison, but they did choose and even work to obtain their perspective. In that moment, they both chose freedom – and instantly became free.

What was the choice which brought such freedom? They chose to love their haters. They chose to look past what the killers were doing and love who they were.

Though they deeply felt the terror of one immersed in the physical and psychological horror of a holocaust, they chose genuine love for everyone – especially those who were horrifically cruel.

From a normal human perspective, to choose love in such a horrifying situation seems illogical, even pathological. From a psychological perspective, however, their constructive response to the atrocities of Auschwitz and Rwanda was not only practical, it was critical to their survival and ultimate success.

This intentionally constructive response enhanced their personal power much more than hate, recrimination, or retribution ever could have. If Viktor Frankl and Immaculée Ilibagiza can successfully achieve peace through the power of a love choice in their extremely desperate circumstances, what does this imply for you and me? What can you and I do when we are feeling captured, arrested, imprisoned, stuck, or overwhelmed? Choose love. This choice is always available to us under any circumstance.

Necessity for the love choice is set up by the simple fact that we are human. We are fallible, flawed creatures who, because of our flaws, hurt each other. Desmond Tutu said it this way, "People are not born hating each other and wishing to cause harm. It is a learned condition."

The movie "42" tells the story of Jackie Robinson (played by Chadwick Boseman), the first black man to play for major league baseball. In a scene from the movie, Jackie takes the field as an angry white crowd yells hateful, racially caustic rejections. A young boy is at the game with his father. The boy seems confused by the emotional intensity around him directed toward the player wearing number 42. He looks up at his screeching red-faced father. The boy hesitates, trying to decide what to do. He mimics the hateful shouts.

Desmond Tutu also said, "In our own ways, we are all broken. Out of that brokenness, we hurt others." Two decades of clinical psychology experience tells me he's right. Hurt is inevitable. Sometimes we give it, sometimes we get it. It's going to happen. When it happens, we have a choice to make.

When hurt, what are our options? If not the love choice, then what? What would be the opposite of love? Hate. The love choice, or the hate choice. What if those were our only options? Who would intentionally choose hate? If we did, how would it be done? Since we are considering it, let's learn from experience just how this hate choice is made.

The Hate Choice - Three Simple Steps

Step One: Assume the Worst

The hate choice requires us to assume the worst. We don't know for sure what people's intentions, perceptions, or motives are, so we can assume malevolent intent.

Look for evidence that they are evil. This is not hard because of "confirmation bias." We tend to see evidence which supports what we already believe, while not noticing contradicting information or interpreting it in a way that supports our belief. We selectively filter evidence in a way that supports our chosen perception.

Are flowers from our hubby evidence that he is trying to hide something? Twelve red roses become twelve read roses. Something can be read into the roses. Don't bother to question assumptions or suspicions; that would get in the way of a hate choice. Roses don't have to be read as an expression of love, they could just as easily be seen as a cover for guilt.

There are upsides and downsides to everything. Magnify the downsides. Focus on the negative. Some percentage of every experience is unpleasant or not to our liking. Expand that part to be the most important part of your perception. Things should have gone differently. Things should have been a lot better than they were. Use the word "should" a lot. Not only should things have been better, they probably are only going to get worse. Make predictions about additional hurt and misdeeds.

Practice paranoia. People are inherently evil. Most people spend a considerable portion of their time trying to make our life miserable. Notice differences between us and them. If they were more like us, things would be better. They are different so don't trust them.

Step Two: Practice Pride

Weird Al Yankovic captured it in "Why Does This Always Happen to Me?" The lyrics depict someone watching television when a special report interrupts the program. A devastating earthquake. Thirty thousand people crushed to death. The television viewer asks, "Why'd they have to interrupt the Simpsons just for this? What a drag cause I was taping it and everything and now I'll have to wait for the rerun to see the part of the show I missed. Why does this always happen to me?"

A good hate choice requires us to over-personalize the offense. It is always about us. The forces of the universe conspire against us to disrupt our life.

The hate choice is about who's right, not so much about what's right. We are right and they, by default, are always wrong.

When someone hurts or offends you, blame them for how you feel. It is all their fault, and you had nothing to do with it. When you get tired of blaming them, blame yourself, but then blame them that you are blaming yourself.

Rent out as much emotional and mental space as possible to whomever offended you, and then blame them for occupying so much space.

You've heard about taking the higher road? Take the "higher than thou" road, and mount your high horse to do it.

Absolutely refuse to forgive – forgiveness totally fouls up the hate choice. It doesn't matter anyway, you can't forgive someone of *this*.

Find out what tribe people belong to. Immaculée Ilibagiza recalls a time in school when students were subjected to ethnic roll call. Not knowing then whether she was Hutu or Tutsi, Immaculée didn't participate in the roll call. Her angry teacher sent her home, forbidding her to return until she knew her tribe. Originally, physical differences distinguished the tribes. After years of living together, marrying each other, and raising mixed-tribe families, physical differences had become minimal and even imperceptible. Because of this, the Hutu-controlled government issued ethnic identification cards so they would know who to hate. When Hutu extremists stopped a driver, he had to show identification. If the card indicated Hutu, he was waved through with approval. If the card identified Tutsi, he got the machete.

Step Three: Think to Destroy

Our mind has the ability to come up with dozens of ways to hurt and destroy. Use your imagination as a tool of destruction.

Demand fairness and justice. In the movie National Treasure, Ben Gates (played by Nicolas Cage) sits with FBI Agent Peter Sadusky (played by Harvey Keitel) after finding the treasure. Sadusky explains two options, both of which result in Ben's going to prison for a long time. Ben would love a solution where he doesn't go to prison. Agent Sadusky replies, "Somebody has to go to prison." That's the idea! You have been wronged. Now someone must go to prison. Fantasize about ways to get even or take revenge. It will feel good to exact vengeance on those who have wronged you.

Value property over people. Exploit people to gain power, prestige, or position.

Trust your fear more than you trust your faith. Let the grievance fester and boil inside of you, fueled by replaying the offense over and over again in your mind. Re-create memories in a way that allows you to hate the offender even more. Create and re-tell a victim story where the offender is the star.

You are justified in taking offense. The hate choice is payback for being mistreated, misunderstood, misquoted, judged, or offended in any variety of ways.

When you choose hate, it makes a lot of difference how you carry yourself. The worst thing you can do is hold your head up and smile, because then you will start to feel better. If you're going to get any satisfaction out of choosing hate, you have to hold on to your misery. Don't cheat yourself of even one moment of feeling miserable.

The Love Choice – Three Simple Steps
Step One: Assume the Best

Assume the best about everyone, especially those who hurt you. We don't know for sure what people's intentions, perceptions, or motives are, so assume they have benevolent intent. Look for evidence that they are good.

Stay positive. How do you feel when life dumps on you? How would you like to feel? Focus right now on any tough situation you are going through. Now, without minimizing what you are facing, consider two ways of looking at it. Things should have been better and are about to get worse (hate choice). Things could have been worse and are about to get better (love choice). Which perspective do you choose? Which gives you the best energy to deal with whatever you are dealing with?

Things are exactly as they should be. According to principles and laws of physics, gravity, cause and effect; the litter on our lawn, our business, and our relationships are exactly where they should be. When litter is launched in a downward thrust toward the lawn, laws of physics take over. Litter ends up exactly where it should. Everything is just as it should be – by law.

People are inherently good. Most people do their best. They do the right thing and make the best choices possible. It could have been me in their spot and them in mine.

Make predictions about healing and forgiveness. Anticipate that others will also make the love choice.

Step Two: Practice Humility

The love choice helps us take things less personally. Rather than "why me," we ask, "why not me?" which is an equally legitimate, but less frequently asked question. The Bible suggests God causes the rain to fall on the just and the unjust. Difficulty and challenge is universal. It happens to, and for, everyone.

We know we're right. It's not that we think we're right, we know we're right. This has us treating each other horribly. We can be absolutely wrong and still know we're right. Exchange being right for being open.

My friend Cam invited me to a fire walk. Even as I filled out the waiver, I figured I was just there to observe this crazy ritual. I know about fire. I know I'm right. As the night unfolds, Cam reiterates, "You can walk on burning coals with bare feet, and your feet remain in perfect condition." My hate-choice reaction to his statement was "Yeah, right!" I know I'm right about fire.

How many times had I walked on fire? Zero. I was proud of that number. How many times had Cam walked on fire? Probably hundreds, and he had taken twenty thousand people across the coals at his events over twenty years. Yet with destructive pride I knew I was right, and he was wrong.

The love choice can feel like stepping onto coals, intentionally acknowledging what we already "know" may be way off. It's a leap of faith. I walked the fire three times that night; first to leap, second to give up being right, and third to embrace being open. What else do I know for sure, about my grievances or limitations, about which I am dead wrong?

Humbly ask, "What is the most loving choice?" Is my choice really a hate choice disguised as a love choice? Bruce is a gay friend who invited us to attend his wedding. With our conservative religious background, my wife and I felt stretched by the prospect of attending. Although we love Bruce, traditional hate choices came up as options. Conveniently, Bruce had chosen the same weekend for his wedding as had our niece. Awesome! Now we can pretend to make a love choice. We would love to go, but our niece's wedding is that same weekend. Everyone understands that we have to put family first. We'll wish Bruce well privately, without the awkwardness of publicly appearing at a gay wedding.

In a perfect turn of events, our niece postpones her wedding, suddenly presenting the choice again. What is the most loving choice? What will people think if we show up? What message do we send our children, grandchildren, friends, neighbors? Pretty good questions. Do I choose love? Or, do I choose hate when I have disapproving opinions about other people's choices? The hate choice sometimes masquerades as a love choice, when really we know somewhere inside of us it is still the hate choice.

Offense is an equal-opportunity opportunity grantor. It gives the offender an opportunity to repent, and the offended an opportunity to forgive. If either does neither, it creates another opportunity for both to do the other.

Step Three: Think to Create

In making the love choice, consider what we can change or control and what we cannot. As acknowledged in the Serenity Prayer, penned by theologian Reinhold Niebuhr:

God, grant me the serenity to accept the things I cannot change, the courage to change the things I can, and wisdom to know the difference.

One thing we can control is our perception. Perception guides our choice about what to do—or not do—about our situation. Do we allow a default (usually negative or hate choice) reaction, or do we choose love?

What happens to us is not nearly as important as how we react to whatever happens to us. We have the power to choose how we see things. From that choice we either build or destroy. Charles Benvegar captured the choice nicely in his poem, "The Wreckers".

> *I watched them tear a building down,*
> *A gang of men in a busy town.*
> *With a ho-heave-ho and lusty yell,*
> *They swung a beam and a sidewall fell.*
>
> *I asked the foreman, "Are these men skilled,*
> *As the men you'd hire if you had to build?"*
>
> *He gave me a laugh and said, "No indeed!*
> *Just common labor is all I need.*
> *I can easily wreck in a day or two*
> *What builders have taken a year to do."*
>
> *I thought to myself as I went my way,*
> *Which of these two roles have I tried to play?*
> *Am I a builder who works with care,*
> *Measuring life by the rule and square?*
> *Am I shaping my deeds by a well-made plan,*
> *Patiently doing the best I can?*
>
> *Or am I a wrecker who walks the town,*
> *Content with the labor of tearing down?*

The magnitude of the hate choice, or of the love choice, can be subtle or severe. There are no neutral choices – it falls on one side or the other, a little or a lot. Unless altered by some contrary force, default is downhill. Mountains erode, buildings crumble, roads deteriorate, and bridges eventually collapse. Rain falls, hits the ground, and flows downhill. Down is default. So it is with our choices.

Without intentional choice, hurt leads to hate. The hate choice requires no effort or positive power.

What do we do with those who love us? Love them! That's easy.

What do we do with those who hate us? Love them! That's hard.

Our mind is built for hard work, and like a well-bred workhorse, the well-trained mind loves tough challenges. As we practice choosing love, it becomes a habit.

Elevation requires lift. Lift requires positive pressure. Sustained positive pressure will get water to flow uphill. Sustained positive effort creates the changes we need. The love choice is higher ground. The view is fantastic. Love lifts and heals hurt. As we firmly, but kindly order our mind to do so, our mind will, after some initial resistance, work very hard to support the love choice. The more painful or difficult the situation, the harder it is to choose love, and the more positively life altering it is when we do so.

Choose love!

About the Author

Dr. Paul Jenkins works with organizations and individuals to establish and maintain habitual patterns of positive perception and focus that increase happiness, engagement, productivity, profit, and ultimate achievement of professional and personal life missions. With two decades of experience as a professional psychologist, Dr. Paul (as he is known to clients and his laughing, learning audiences) lays out the how and the why behind the art and science of being constructive in an often destructive environment. It is like having an owner's manual for your brain – one you can actually read, understand, and apply. You understand your own mind and improve its functioning on purpose.

His deeply thoughtful writing, engaging and fun keynote addresses, powerfully practical breakout seminars, individual and corporate coaching and counseling are profound and simple. His clients, readers, and audiences get an iron grip on powerful psychological principles that make an immediate difference in their personal, family, and professional lives.

Dr. Paul's book *Pathological Positivity* and its pocket-sized companion *Portable Positivity*, are available now to power up your positivity. Corporate and group discounts can be arranged to provide these books to all members of your organization.

www.PathologicalPositivity.com
www.PortablePositivity.com

Paul H. Jenkins, Ph.D.
Positivity Psychologist
Live On Purpose
1429 South 550 East, Orem, UT 84097
801-380-5161
Info@DrPaulJenkins.com
www.DrPaulJenkins.com
facebook.com/pathologicalpositivity
drpauljenkins

LIVE ON PURPOSE

The Red Thread of Relationships

by Dr. Russ Gaede

THE RIGHT RELATIONSHIP, consistently nurtured, will transform your life. We often do not realize the ways we influence others. A Chinese Proverb states, "An invisible red thread connects those who are destined to meet regardless of time, place, or circumstance. The thread may stretch or tangle, but it will never break." Think for a moment, with whom are you connected with the red thread? Who are you destined to meet, and more importantly, influence? We do not know, but we can be an influence to everyone we meet.

When we influence others, we are sharing a part of ourselves. When we share a part of ourselves by expressing appreciation, we are showing others that they have value. Helping others realize their value shows our love for them. Every one of us has value. We may not always see our value or someone else's value right away. Take time to find and acknowledge the value in yourself and others. It may take a few minutes or sometimes years before we realize the value others have shared and how it has affected our lives.

I learned a great life lesson from two boys that changed my life forever, but did not realize it until years later. I believe the boys and I were connected by a red thread. There were some twists and tangles in our relationship, but ultimately, a change was made in all of our lives.

I have Tourette syndrome (TS), a neurological disorder characterized by repetitive, stereotyped, involuntary movements (motor tics) and vocalizations (verbal tics). Since a young age, I have had tics, both motor and verbal. Sometimes I would sit at the kitchen table doing homework and before writing I would have to shake my arm. Other times, when talking to people I would stutter a little before I could say what I was trying to say. Vocally, I would clear my throat or make a guttural sound and scrunch my nose while sniffing.

One of the difficulties came because I did not know why I had tics and vocalized. I have a name for my difficulties now, but back then, I had not even heard of Tourette syndrome. All I knew was when people asked, "Why do you do that?" I would respond with "Do what?" because I did not realize I was doing anything "weird." My other response, when I realized what I was doing, was to say, "I just do" and brush it off externally. Internally, I was holding on to the difficulty.

The other difficulty came because no one else around me knew why I had tics either. I was often told to "stop it" of "knock it off." I believe that others thought I was ticking on purpose to be irritating. When I would attempt to "stop it," the tension created by the need to tic built within me making it worse when they came out. This all played a part in lowering my self-esteem.

My belief system told me that because I had tics, my value was very low and I would not make much of myself because I was "defective." Although I still do not have control over my tics, I have changed my belief system. I understand that Tourette syndrome does not and will not keep me from the success for which I strive.

For many years I attempted to ignore the fact that I had tics which I could not control. I was embarrassed and would get irritated if anyone ever brought up my tics. In fact, when people brought it up, I would sometimes shut down and not talk to them anymore. I was in my mid-twenties when I was diagnosed with Tourette syndrome. Although it was a relief to finally put a diagnoses with my involuntary behavior, it still was difficult to talk about and discuss with others.

I was attending the University of Utah, working toward earning my bachelor's degree in psychology, when I finally came to understand the diagnosis and learn to live with it rather than fight against it. While attending the University of Utah, I learned about Tourette in my classes and started putting the pieces together.

I began interacting with two professors, Dr. Bill Henry and Dr. Sally Ozanoff, who helped me learn that having Tourette syndrome was not a bad thing from which to hide. Dr. Bill Henry was one of my psychology professors. I would spend time in his office talking and seeking help with my school work. As we spent time talking, we began to form a relationship that was supportive and helpful. We then began discussing my Tourette syndrome.

Dr. Sally Ozanoff was researching Tourette syndrome at the time. Dr. Henry introduced us and she would often join Dr. Henry while we discussed Tourette syndrome.

As I worked with Drs. Henry and Ozanoff, the red thread that tied us together was strengthened. They helped me come to grips with having Tourette syndrome. I learned that my value was not dependent on whether I had tics or not. They encouraged me to seek out a diagnosis so I could put a name to what I was experiencing. I agreed and made an appointment to see a doctor. After collecting my history, I was diagnosed with moderate to severe Tourette syndrome. Finally, I could begin explaining what was going on when others asked.

While I was attending the University of Utah and working with the professors, I was also working at the Boys and Girls Club as a youth counselor. I specifically worked with nine- and ten-year-old youth. Built in 1968, the club is located on the edge of a city park. It is a beautiful setting. We would often be outside at the park interacting as a group. The boys and girls of the club came from many walks of life and socio-economic backgrounds as it serviced six elementary schools. Ages of the youth in the part of the club I worked in ranged from eight to twelve years of age. I enjoyed my work as I was able to help the youth in which I came in contact.

Having Tourette and working with nine- and ten-year-old youth was not always a good combination. There were two boys, who were good friends, which were under my responsibility that were quite a challenge at times. These two boys were very active and teased other youth in the club. When we would have a quiet activity or lesson, they would find it difficult sitting still and would talk with each other. I did not let the boys know they were challenging. I enjoyed working with them and helping them achieve what they set out to do. I believe we had a positive relationship.

The youth in the club would often ask why I ticked and sometimes make fun of me. When asked, I would change the subject and ultimately not answer their question. I became good at re-directing conversations.

Drs. Henry and Ozanoff encouraged me to discuss my Tourette syndrome with the boys and girls at the club. I was very hesitant at first as I feared the reaction of the youth and felt that my ticks would be more noticeable. After long discussion with the professors and them helping me realize the benefits of talking more openly about Tourette syndrome, I took their advice and decided to let the boys and girls know why I had motor and vocal tics.

When I was ready to tell the boys and girls at the club, I took them all into a room and discussed my Tourette. Not only was my group in the room, I also invited all the groups and their leaders. I was totally out of my comfort zone. I explained Tourette syndrome, showed a video about how it affects people, and then I let them ask questions. The discussion went well and I was relieved to have it over. After all the questions were answered, I told them that we would not discuss it again and that my Tourette would be a non-issue.

The next day I was standing in the game room and I had a facial motor tic. There were several youth around me who were in the discussion the day before, including these two boys. As I ticked, two young girls that were standing in front of me began teasing me. Before I could say anything to the two girls, the two young boys walked up from behind me, looked at the two girls who were teasing me and said, "Knock it off, we talked about this yesterday," then looked at me and smiled. The bond we had was strengthened between us. I learned that being open and honest in relationships and by sharing my struggles strengthened the red thread that binds us all together.

These two boys showed me the love I needed in that situation. They influenced me in ways they may never realize. It took me years to recognize how they influenced my life for good. The reason they felt comfortable in standing up for me, an adult, was because of the relationship we had formed. They realized that we all have differences. Just because my differences are not the same as yours doesn't mean we can't still help and strengthen each other.

We show love to others by influencing them to do good, be good, and achieve good. Love is more than a feeling, it is an action word, a word that we choose to express. We can express our love by helping each other be the best we can be.

The red thread is strengthened by individuals interacting and making a difference in each other's lives. Swiss psychiatrist and psychotherapist Carl Jung (1875-1961) said, "The meeting of two personalities is like the contact of two chemical substances: if there is any reaction, both are transformed." I believe that every contact we have affects each person involved. We may not see the transformation, but each of us are changed even if only in a small simple way.

We connect with people every day. How do you show you care about those with whom you connect? Do you make every connection about what they can do for you or what you can do for them? Showing love and kindness creates a positive transformation to all involved. We all have something to share and to gain from the relationships we create. When we are looking for the positives in our connections, we will find the positives. We attract what we seek and focus on.

There is power in relationships and connecting that we often do not realize. Learn to share the benefits of relationships with others. Be open and honest with them by sharing how they help you and show your appreciation to them.

Think for a moment, whose life are you influencing?

When we influence others, we are learning how to collaborate. Collaboration is the act of working with someone to create something better. Collaboration takes time and often takes effort. What are you willing to do to create a positive, collaborative relationship that shows your love and concern for others? The way the professors and I collaborated gave me the trust in them that what they were advising me to do was for the best, and it was for the best.

As we learn to collaborate with and help others, we become a person others seek out. People seek out those they trust and value. We become people who are trusted and valued when, as Stephen Covey said, "Seek first to understand, then to be understood." Be a person that listens and finds out how you can help others.

You are in charge of your own destiny. You choose how to respond when a challenge or difficulty is placed in your path. Reaching out to others through relationships can strengthen us and help us overcome our struggles. The process of connecting and collaborating is what defines our relationships.

There are many inspiring stories of people who have overcome seemingly insurmountable odds. Those who successfully triumph over their adversities are able to live a productive life instead of surrendering to difficulties. The relationships in their lives helped them achieve their potential. Choose to do the same!

Some of these great individuals include Abraham Lincoln who had several setbacks and what some people call "failures" before and after being the President of the United States. He suffered from depression, lost his wife to death, and experienced several defeats in his attempts to become a congressman. Abraham Lincoln said, "I am a success today because I had a friend who believed in me and I didn't have the heart to let him down."

Bethany Hamilton is a professional surfer who lost her arm during a shark attack. After the attack and much practice and persistence, she continued to compete. She had several top 5 finisher events, including many where she took first place. The love and support from her family helped her achieve more than she thought she could after the accident.

Oprah Winfrey grew up in poverty and suffered years of abuse. She became a single teen mother at the age of 14. Although she experienced many hardships, she became the president of Harpo Productions and a billionaire. She once said, "Everyone wants to ride with you in the limo, but what you want is someone who will take the bus with you when the limo breaks down." What kind of person are you? Are you willing to ride the bus when a friend's limo breaks down?

Victor Frankl is a Holocaust survivor and author of two amazing books on living life to its fullest and overcoming the trials in his life. "Life is never made unbearable by circumstances, but only by lack of meaning and purpose." Remember that the difficulties you experience are bearable with help from a friend.

Many others have overcome what appears to be the impossible. Can your name be added to the list of those who have overcome?

Vivian Green said, "Life isn't about waiting for the storm to pass, it's about learning to dance in the rain." Make the choice to dance in the rain. In other words, choose to work through your adversity rather than fighting against it or surrendering to it.

I began learning to dance in the rain when I decided that my Tourette syndrome does not define me. How I handled my difficulties defined me. I made a conscious decision to change my belief systems and behaviors to mirror others who have successfully overcome their adversity. I was helped by two great professors and two ten-year-old boys. Who will you allow to help you through tough times and difficulty? Who will you help?

Marianne Williamson said, "Our deepest fear is not that we are inadequate. Our deepest fear is that we are powerful beyond measure. It is our light, not our darkness that most frightens us. We ask ourselves, 'Who am I to be brilliant, gorgeous, talented, fabulous?' Actually, who are you not to be? You are a child of God. Your playing small does not serve the world. There is nothing enlightened about shrinking so that other people won't feel insecure around you. We are all meant to shine, as children do. We were born to make manifest the glory of God that is within us. It's not just in some of us; it's in everyone. And as we let our own light shine, we unconsciously give other people permission to do the same. As we are liberated from our own fear, our presence automatically liberates others."

I thought I was inadequate, but I was wrong. I feared the unknown so I hid myself thinking I was worthless. I have learned that I shouldn't play small simply because I fear what might happen. I am a story in the making and so are you. As I have been liberated from my own fear, I hope to liberate others.

Show love and appreciation to those around you by letting your light shine.

About the Author

Dr. Russell Gaede's life is an inspiring example of how to overcome obstacles and reach your potential.

Dr. Russ went from High School drop out to becoming a college professor with a Doctorate in Psychology. As a kid, he was in leg braces and had a difficult time running - he has since gone to become an avid cyclist and long distance runner who has biked and run tens of thousands of miles.

Having struggled with severe speech impediments and a diagnoses of Tourette Syndrome, Dr. Russ now makes his living as a speaker, author and coach.

Dr. Russ is a successful entrepreneur having built a million dollar business as a therapist. He is the author of multiple books and has been featured on various TV and radio programs.

In his speeches, Dr. Russ shares hilarious and inspiring stories that teach the principles he has used in his life to overcome adversity and achieve success.

Russell C. Gaede, PsyD
Author, Speaker, Coach
Regenesys, Inc
801-410-1671
drrussspeaks@gmail.com
www.drrussspeaks.com
www.facebook.com/drrussspeaks
@dr_russspeaks

NATIONAL SPEAKERS ASSOCIATION

NSA

MOUNTAIN WEST
Idaho, Montana, Utah, Wyoming

Serving Engineers Some Love – One Chocolate Chip Cookie at a Time!

by Sydne Jacques

TWENTY YEARS AGO I made the decision to leave a very stable (but also kind of boring) government job with incredible benefits and start my own business. In the past 20 years I have built a multi-million dollar, award-winning engineering firm. I am a unique individual—I am most often called "an engineer with a personality" sounds like an oxymoron doesn't it?

When I started my business the first thing that I learned is that every one of us is asking the same question. Even though our industries and our businesses are different, we are all asking the same question: **What can we do that will differentiate us from our competition?**

I know that for me, once I had my business license in hand, these are the things that I was asking: "What am I going to do to create demand for my engineering services? What can we do as a company that will differentiate us? There are so many successful engineering firms – what can I do that will set us apart?"

I don't think it matters if your business is an engineering firm, a restaurant, a hotel, or a direct sales company – we all need to ask ourselves the same question. We all have competition and the only way to stay in business and be profitable is to figure out what we are going to do different than our competition. What can we offer that will set us apart? How can we serve our customers so that we will stand out and they will remember us and want to work with our company over and over again? How do we differentiate ourselves from the competition? That's the golden question.

One of my greatest discoveries is the answer to that question! I have utilized these principles to not only build my engineering firm, but I have also used this same model to build two successful non-profit organizations. There really are no limits for the application of this discovery!

It was in 1994 when I obtained a business license and starting building my engineering firm. At that point in time I had a few years experience working as an engineer, but as I looked around at other successful companies I was actually a little scared. It seemed that every other engineering firm had more experience than I did, they all had better connections, and quite honestly, it seemed like an incredibly hard industry in which a young female engineer could make her mark.

But I was optimistic and determined and I kept moving forward. As I worked on my business plan there were many questions that needed to be answered – but the one that kept me awake at night was, "What can we do that will differentiate us from our competition?"

I'm sure I wasn't the first business owner to ask that question, and the more I thought about it, the more I realized that every business should be asking the very same question.

I started to think about the restaurants that we liked to frequent. What did they do that made them different from the others? I started paying crazy attention to every business where I spent money – when I bought groceries, filled my car with gas, stayed at a hotel on vacation, or even when I took my kids to the dentist. I started to understand that all of us were trying to figure out how to stay in business, how to serve our customers, how to stay profitable, and ultimately, how to differentiate ourselves from our competition.

Do you remember what the world was like in 1994? There was no Amazon, no Zappos, no Google. As I looked at the successful businesses, Walmart was at the top of the list. At that point in time they had just started having greeters at the door. They were known for excellent customer service. If you asked any employee where something was, they would immediately walk you to that item to ensure that you could find what you were looking for.

As I was working on my business plan and striving to learn how other companies distinguish themselves, I made an incredible discovery! I discovered something that I wished they taught in business school; I discovered what I now call the "Upper Arrow."

If you really get this – this will change your whole business – and this will change your customer service strategy. I am 100% certain that if you understand and implement the "Demand Diagram," it will change your company culture and it will change your bottom line.

It's a pretty simple diagram. On one axis you have Customer Satisfaction, and on the other axis you have Quality. This is the quality of your product and service, what I call your customer experience, and this is what you deliver to your customers.

Now what they teach you in business school is exactly true, as the quality of your experience goes up, customer satisfaction goes up as well. We all know this, right? What they don't teach you is what happens next. At a certain point you go into a state of diminishing returns. You can continue to increase the quality of your experience, but the customer is not going to notice all your efforts, and the increase in quality is not going to result in an increase in customer satisfaction.

Let's think about the airlines for a minute. If my airline promises me that they will get me to my destination within 5 minutes of my scheduled time, this makes me happy, and I am a satisfied customer. But if they work really, really hard and continue to increase that quality so they can get me there within 1 minute of the scheduled time – will I be more satisfied? No – it doesn't matter to me, because I will be waiting for my bags. This is what we call the point of diminishing returns. For each of us, no matter what experience we provide, we all reach a point that if we continue to work really hard to improve the quality of the customer experience, it is NOT going to result in increased satisfaction for our customers.

So when it comes to the airlines, some of them have figured out that they have to do something different so their customers will be truly delighted and their customer satisfaction will continue to move up on the demand diagram, or what I have named the "Upper Arrow." What can they do to set themselves apart? What can they do so their customers are not only "satisfied", but "loyal"? For me, I am all about the frequent flier programs. I was thrilled to discover that I can earn a permanent companion pass on Southwest Airlines. Every time I fly I can take someone with me for free. That is an Upper Arrow that Southwest offers that keeps me extremely satisfied as a customer and keeps me very loyal to their airline.

So, back to my quest to build a successful business. I am a brand new business owner. I have a few years experience as an engineer, and I have a decent reputation, but I looked at all these other competitors that had more experience than me, with more years on the job and with better connections. How could I differentiate myself? And how could I create real demand? Have you ever had that thought before?

As I pondered these questions, I thought about the diagram and the Upper Arrow. The Upper Arrow is what sets you apart; it's what jumps over the diminishing returns, it's what exponentially improves the experience for the customer, and it's that uniqueness that nobody else offers that differentiates you. And I wondered what that could be for me?

And then I start to think back on some life experiences that I have had. When I was a brand new engineer, my first job was with the Forest Service. During my first year of working there, I was invited to attend a training at 3M

Company to learn to become a Total Quality Management facilitator. I went to Minneapolis for a 5-day training session. Our training was at an Embassy Suites hotel; a very nice facility with incredible customer service. The highlight of the day happened every day, right around 3:00 in the afternoon, when a cute older gentleman would come through the back door wearing a white baker's apron. He brought warm chocolate chip cookies, and we all looked forward to it every day. But on Friday, the last day of our class, we all started looking at the back door at around 3 p.m. But do you know what happened that day? There were no chocolate chip cookies. It was a crushing defeat. We were all so disappointed, and I remember thinking to myself that day that **every class or every meeting is always better with fresh-baked chocolate chip cookies.**

So years later as I was working on my business plan, I determined my Upper Arrow! I love to bake chocolate chip cookies, most people love to eat chocolate chip cookies—that's it! Yep, chocolate chip cookies would be my point of distinction. I decided from that time forward, I would bring chocolate chip cookies to all my meetings. That set me apart because in the engineering world, guess how many other firms give their clients home-baked chocolate chip cookies? Most engineers don't even know how to make a tasty chocolate chip cookie, let alone commit to get up extra early every morning to make cookies for meetings so that they would be fresh every single day.

So as part of my business plan I included a company commitment to provide chocolate chip cookies as my Upper Arrow, and then I started baking cookies. Every time that I hired a new employee, I personally performed the employee orientation, and a very important part of the orientation was making sure that each new employee understood the Upper Arrow and our commitment to providing a quality product and service for our clients, topped off by the added value of fresh baked chocolate chip cookies at every meeting, workshop or conference that we attended. At the end of every employee orientation, I would teach them how to make our chocolate chip cookies so they were always soft and consistently delicious, no matter which employee from our firm brought them to the meeting.

Of course, our success didn't happen overnight. Building a successful business takes a lot of time and hard work. But soon the word got out. Some of the contracts that we obtain are by low-bid, but the majority of the work we do is selection-based. Many times we partner with larger firms as a subconsultant, and I know for a fact that when people are trying to decide who to partner with, they at least sometimes think of our cookies. They know that we have the skills and experience to offer a quality service just like our competitors, but they also know that we bring a bonus – home-baked refreshments for every meeting, for the entire length of the project. We have created a type of synergy; I love baking cookies, and our clients love eating them.

So twenty years ago, I started building my engineering firm with homemade cookies as my Upper Arrow. I can tell you story after story about successful deals and successful projects, and many of them came about because people love to work with someone who brings chocolate chip cookies to every meeting. I also believe it isn't just because we all like to consume chocolate chip cookies, but others know it is how we share our company's love. We don't just stop by the grocery store before a meeting and pick out some donuts or cookies from the bakery, we get up early and bake those cookies every morning so they are always fresh. We ran some calculations and figured out that last year as an organization we baked over 20,000 cookies! That is a lot of love that we share with engineers, contractors and the teams that we work with every day.

When I showed my friend Kevin Miller the Upper Arrow he said, "You and I are teaching the same principle! I always say there are two parts to truly serving a customer; first solve their problem, then do something to make them feel good."

Yes, that Upper Arrow – that's the part that should make your customer feel good, or better yet, make them feel great! When your customers feel great because of the experience that you provide, they will go from feeling satisfied to being loyal to you. And loyal customers tend to tell others about their positive experiences, and that is what we business owners live for!

I love teaching these principles! I love working with companies to help them discover how they can differentiate themselves and create loyal customers. So my question to you is, "what is your Upper Arrow?" Can you identify what it is for your organization? How about for the company division in which you work? Or better yet, what is the Upper Arrow for you personally? Do you know? Will you take time to figure it out?

There are multiple ways that I have applied the principle of the Upper Arrow. Let me briefly describe two more ways. The first is within our company; each year every employee is encouraged to select an "Upper Arrow project" that they can perform to add value to the company. This project is something above and beyond their regular job description, but is something that they chose for themselves. Usually it is something that they are passionate about that will make them even more engaged at work because they get to spend time on something of their own choosing.

As an example, Carin, my office manager, has run more than 40 marathons and is more fit than the rest of us put together! Last year she decided to organize a wellness program for our company for her Upper Arrow contribution. She ordered pedometers for employees and their families. We recorded our steps, had contests, shared healthy recipes, and, of course, had prizes. It was a fantastic program and we all loved it! It was a win/win for all who participated. Carin was

165

excited to share her passion for wellness and every employee and their family benefited from her efforts.

As another example, Scott is one of my project managers. Before he came to work for me, he used to own his own construction company with an average of 300 employees on his payroll. He is an absolute genius with spreadsheets. For one of his "Upper Arrow projects," he created a brand-new, industry-specific project management tool. It not only helps us track our activities and our data, but we use this amazing tool to generate visual reports for our clients every month that shows our current progress with the schedule and the budget. Our clients love it! Scott is proud of what he created, and he is always excited to train new employees on how to use it. We have improved client relationships because of his effort. The whole organization benefits when each employee chooses an "Upper Arrow project" each year.

The last application of the Upper Arrow that I want to share with you is how we can each personally take time to decide on our own personal Upper Arrow, something that we can do to be more valuable and to contribute more to others. Let me give you two ideas to consider.

Years ago I was listening to the radio and they were interviewing a man that was turning 103 years old! The radio announcer was asking all kinds of questions – what do you eat? What have you done for exercise all these years? How much water do you drink? Do you take supplements? The gentleman listened patiently and answered, "Long, long ago I figured out the secret to life. Would you like to hear it?"

The announcer answered in the affirmative. The man then said, "My secret to life is that every day I get out of bed, I look out the window, and then I say out loud, 'Oh, this is just the kind of day I was hoping for!'"

I have learned that sometimes it is snowy outside, sometimes rainy, sometimes cloudy and sometimes it's a beautiful sunshiny day. But I have learned that no matter what is happening on the outside, I can still choose to make it a great day on the "inside." I love his advice! I learned long ago that I can choose to have a good attitude no matter what happens to me. I can always choose to be happy and treat others with love. Choosing to always have a good attitude could be an Upper Arrow that would bring you higher energy and set you apart from the average person.

Here is one more idea of a personal Upper Arrow. When I started my business about 20 years ago, I hired a coach to give me some advice and to help me set up a business plan. He taught me a lot of great things, but the one thing that I will never forget is that he was constantly teaching me to be "100% present." He promised me that if I would learn to be 100% present with people, I would succeed in my business. Think back to twenty years ago when he was teaching me this: I didn't have a laptop, a cell phone, an iPod or belonged to any social media. None of those distractions even existed, and yet his number one piece of advice was to be 100% present. Now, more than ever as individuals, as team members, as leaders, as parents – we need to strive to be 100% present in the presence of other people.

I have a little trick I use…it's called a trigger…to help me remember. It started because whenever I came home from work, I wanted to put my phone away and be 100% present when I would walk through the door and enter the presence of my family. Now when I walk through other doors, I think to myself, "who is on the other side of this door? Who do I get the privilege to see, to converse with and to learn from? How can I serve others? Who can I be 100% present with?"

Don't you agree, that if you and I choose to be 100% present with the people with whom we are around, that can also be an Upper Arrow that will set us apart from the crowd?

I love the concept of the Upper Arrow! I hope that you will utilize the power of the Upper Arrow in your organization, on your teams and in your personal life. And if you want, feel free to copy my model and start sharing the love — one chocolate chip cookie at a time.

About the Author

After several years of working as a civil engineer for the government, Sydne Jacques decided to abandon her cubicle, go out on her own and founded Jacques & Associates. By applying the business principles that she teaches audiences today, she has built a multi-million dollar, award-winning engineering firm.

In addition to serving as CEO of Jacques and Associates, Sydne has founded two non-profit organizations, is a member of the National Speakers Association, is a Senior Facilitator with the International Partnering Institute and currently sits on the National Advisory Board for the College of Engineering at Brigham Young University.

Sydne has a unique set of skills – she is a professional engineer with an engaging personality and has strengths and certifications in facilitation and communication. Sydne brings her more than 20 years of entrepreneurial success and leadership acumen to every speech to help business leaders understand how to excel and create distinction.

Whether she is speaking to entrepreneurs, leaders or frontline employees, Sydne's insights into leadership, marketing and customer service are practical, proven and powerful. She is the creator of the Upper Arrow Model, which has been described by clients as "what they should have taught us in business school." It is the understanding of the Upper Arrow Principle that put her company on the map and has allowed it to thrive for more than 20 years. When she's not speaking, or in the kitchen baking those famous chocolate chip cookies that are her trademark, she loves to spend time on the basketball court.

Sydne grew up on a farm in Montana and will always claim she was raised by the best parents in the world. She is grateful for parents that taught her how to work hard, and helped her believe she could accomplish whatever she set her mind to. Sydne has been married to Darryl Jacques for 25 years and has four awesome kids who are the highlight of her life.

Sydne Jacques
Engineer With A Personality
331 N 280 W, Orem UT 84057
801-358-8923
sydne@upperarrow.com
www.upperarrow.com

Just Love It!

by Tannen Graham

IN 1988 NIKES "Just Do It" marketing campaign launched to increase its share of the sport-shoe business. This campaign is one of the top two taglines of the 20th century being both intensely personal and universal! The "Just Do It" campaign spoke to people regardless of age, gender, wealth, or physical fitness level which led Nike to become one of the most well-recognized brands in the world as these three words went global.

The statement "Just Do It" spread like wildfire and went way beyond athletes. Although, athletes like Michael Jordan and Kobe Bryant were seen wearing Nike Just do it Tee shirts, along with tennis start Roger Federer and many other famous spots. Then outdoor billboards, print media and even graffiti artist started using this famous saying cementing Nikes image as an innovative American icon, the normal every day person also claimed these famous three words as their own personal mantra.

I personally have used "Just Do it" to talk myself into getting out of bed, going to work, balancing my checkbook, starting the laundry, and even to write this book. I've been told that the saying has given courage to others while asking for a date, talking to a girl, walking down the isle, asking for a raise, and I even had a Director of HR tell me when preparing to terminate someone from their position she would take a deep breath in and think "Just do it" before pulling the plug on the soon to be unemployed employee. Once, I over heard a six your old say to her little sister, "Just Do It" pull off the bandage! I guess, when uttering these three little words our courage is kick-stared and the task at hand can begin. These three words can catapult you from dipping your toe in the water to jumping in headfirst.

The question then becomes, what happens after speaking or saying these famous three words out load or just in our minds? So you've asked for a raise, you asked someone out on a date, you took the first step of that three-mile run, you said no to your boss for the first time ever, you ran on the field in front of millions, you overcame your fear of public speaking and took the mic and began speaking. What happens next?

By all accounts declaring you are just "going to do it" only takes three seconds. But what follows most likely will take much much longer. How do you keep the faith, the drive, or the passion alive once you have started? Well, right after I say "Just Do IT" I back it up with now "Just Love it!" Why just love it? Love is a very powerful emotion. It has started wars, ended careers, and pushed people to do things they never thought possible. Love makes us laugh and even cry, sometimes at the same time. It drives us mentally crazy, yet it can drive us crazy (if you know what I mean). Love can make us patient, or impatient. Love endorse time, yet leaves us wanting more time to love. You can be love someone, yet not be in-love with someone. Love has so many levels, its almost hard to explain.

When talking about work, chore's, task's or our careers, it's hard to consider using the word love. But, if you love what you do, or at least a have personal respect for it, it just seems easier. If you hate what you are doing, or dread what you are doing it seems to take twice as long and be twice as hard. I'm not saying you have to be in love with firing someone, saying no to someone, or even love the process of overcoming your deepest fears. What I am saying it adding hatred or loathing to any task will make the task harder every time.

The ancient Greeks have a very sophisticated way of talking about love. They recognized six different varieties of love so as not to be cruel and use one word for all things that might describe love. Romantic love, albeit nice is not the only kind of love I'm speaking of when I say "Just Love It!"

They say the first kind of love was **Eros**, named after the Greek God of fertility and it represented the idea of sexual passion and desire. In today's world we think of love as something positive, in the past, Eros was viewed as fiery, dangerous, and a form of irrational love. It could take a hold of you and possess you causing you to lose all control.

Philia, or deep friendship; which the Greeks and most of us would value far more than the out of control crazy love known as Eros. Defined as a love of deep friendships and comradely developed between brothers in arms, teammates, fellow survivors, and even folks in the same congregation, or those fighting for the same cause. This is where loyalty to your friends, sacrificing for your children, sharing your good days or your bad days would reside. This is different than amassing followers on Facebook or twitter, I really don't see the Greeks being impressed with our social form of Philia.

Ludus, or playful love refers to the affection between children or young lovers. Most of us over the age of 12 have had a taste of flirting or teasing while around our friends or when meeting new people at a party. Have you ever danced with strangers and had the time of your life, well I have and it's the closes example to Ludus love I could find.

Ah, **Agape**, or love for everyone or selfless love. Apage is the love you extend to all people whether they are family members or distant stranger. C.S. Lewis refers to it as "gift love" and the highest form of Christian love. Buddhism uses the word "metta' to describe "universal loving kindness" which is close to Agape. I believe the world would be a better place if we would renew our capability to care and/or love everyone Agape.

Pragma, or long-standing love is the deepest understanding and development between long-married couples. Making compromises, showing patience, giving love not just receiving it, and creating tolerance is the true definition of Pargma or "standing in love."

Philautia, love of the self comes in two forms one of the unhealthy variety associated with obsession, narcissism, and focusing on fame and fortune, where you become completely self absorbed. A healthier version enhances your capability to love deeply, feel secure, be self compassionate, or as Aristotle put it "All friendly feelings for others are an extension of a man's feelings for himself".

None of us like difficulties, going against the grain, getting pushing back, being left behind, or making hard decisions. If we had a choice, we probably wouldn't go through them. But believe it or not our challenges past and present have a purpose. They are in fact preparing us for our future. We all need to learn to love our mistakes no matter how big or small they are.

Discovering the importance of loving setback, each moment of pain, every "I can't do this", "this will never work" and understand you experienced them to enrich your life is what I hope reading this book will due.

When you're always thinking about the tough times, the times it didn't work out for you, the times you wish you had done something more, something less or the time you just gave up, thinking about these things over and over just brings more of the same. When you look back over your life and some of the things that you faced was there ever a time where you didn't think you'd make it through? Where the obstacles looked too big? Maybe the medical report was bad, the breakup left a the hole in your heart, you didn't get the promotion you deserved, maybe you couldn't see a way where anything would ever work out in your favor.

Have you ever met someone going through the exact same things as you are only they come out smiling while you feel like crying? Have you ever met someone who truly is worse off than you maybe they just lost their job, they don't have a lot of money, they been told they have a terminal illness yet they smile they even joke around when they should be serious, and they even seem happier than you? I think it's because they've learned how to "Just Love It!" no matter what the (it) is.

It's important to note when I say "just Love it" I'm not putting down the importance of a bad medical report, the pain of losing a job, the devastation of losing a loved one, or anything else that life might throw at you but I am saying is it's your choice how you process it. It's an age-old saying it's not how many times you get knocked down its how many times you get back up. But if you get back up and your tainted, soured, depressed, or don't give a damn, what's the point in getting back up again?

Instead of being discouraged consider reviewing your past and remember that it got you to this point. It's up to you if your past will repeat itself. Just know that what you give focus to gross. Meaning if every morning you get up and say "it's going to be a great day" or "it's going to be an awful day" you can already guess what type of day you are going to have. At this point a lot of people say to me Tannen, just don't know my spouse, or you just don't know my boss, or you just don't know my children, and there's more I also hear Tannen, you don't understand how hard I work, you have no idea how broke I am, and the doctor told me I'm not doing so well.

To which I always reply the following way: Just Love your spouse or someone else will! Just Love that job, or someone else will. Just Love those children because no matter how much they might be driving you crazy there are thousands of couples who cant have children who would Love to have the troubles children bring today. Love the fact you have work to do and are able to do it. When people talk to me about being broke I cant help myself and feel compelled to ask them a few qualifying questions such as "are you complaining about money while sitting in your home, watching NetFlix, or driving your car, or calling me from an iPhone, because I am positive I could find someone who is only dreaming of having those things one day – so are you broke, or are you just a little financially challenged at the moment. As for medical reports, I am married to a doctor and have the up-most respect for them and the services they provide, but they do not have the last word when it comes to you and your health.

I guess what I'm saying is don't complain about the problem because in complaining your energy is focused on the problem and not on the solution. Example if you're sick and tired of being sick and tired and all you talk about is being sick and tired all you're going to get is more being sick and tired. However, should you wake up tomorrow and have a different mindset, a healthier mindset and say to yourself today I feel great, today my body feels healthy and strong, today I'm craving healthy whole foods, today water is my drink of choice and you actually thought this way all day long I promise you would start to see a change. It's common knowledge you can't think to thoughts at one time. Go ahead try it, try being mad and happy at the same time. You can't one moment you can be mad, and the next moment you could be happy, but not at the same time. So, with this simple logic if you created a healthy mindset and only think healthy thoughts your mind, body, and spirit would have to follow.

When you get down, feel defeated, can't possibly see a way how you're ever going to get better, how you ever going to get out of debt, how you will ever meet the person of your dreams, go back and remember to Just Love It -whatever you've been through and know your best days are still ahead of you if you can find a way to Just Love It and not hate it. Maybe remembering when where you were in the right place at the right time to help someone else out, when someone helped you out, when you found front row parking, when you found the perfect present for someone you love, when out of the blue someone buys your cup of coffee, or you found out the water heater you needed to replace just went on sale.

These are the little things in life we may not even notice when we are focusing on what we don't want instead of on what we do want. On what we love vs what we hate. If we are always talking about how bad our life is, instead of how great live is, we might miss these mini miracles that take place every hour of every day. We might not notice the paperboy taken extra time to deliver paper right side up. We might not notice the lady at the dry cleaners double checking our shirts for cleanliness. If we fail to see others all around us working to make our lives better how could we do the same? If we don't do the same and stay weighted down, feeling alone, we are missing the main point of life. If we don't support something bigger than ourselves we may miss catching the love that others have for us. Being in service of others is one of the best ways to start feeling better. I have a few simple

While doing research for this book I ran across the 10 keys to Happier living written by Action For Happiness and I truly believe if you can find a way ot "Just Love it" happiness is possible.

Here's what they had to say. Everyone's path to Love and happiness is different but the research suggest these 10 things consistently tend to have a positive impact on people's overall happiness and well-being. The first five relate to how we interact with the outside world in our daily activities. The second five come from more of and inside love and depend on our attitude to life.

1. **Giving:** Simply do things for others. Giving is better than receiving.

2. **Relating:** Connect with people. Not with machines. Face-booking and tweeting don't count. Face to face, eye-to-eye connection never goes out in style.

3. **Exercising:** Taking care of your body is crucial because it's only when you get.

4. **Appreciating:** Notice the world around you, consider the power of Mother Nature, and notice the people supporting you.

5. **Trying out:** Keep learning new things, if you stop growing you start dying.

6. **Direction:** Have goals to look forward to, if you don't know where you are you don't know where you can go.

7. **Resilience:** Find ways to bounce back, use the mantra "Just Love It"

8. **Emotion:** Take a positive approach.

9. **Acceptance:** Be comfortable with who you are, you are one of a kind.

10. **Meaning:** Be a part of something bigger, be of service before being served.

Actions for Happiness also goes on to write six things to consider practicing daily. I have these posted on my mirror in my bathroom so I can see them daily. Remember with love all things are possible.

1. **Daily mindfulness:** the present and accepting. Mindfulness is another way of paying attention to the present moment when we become aware of our thoughts and feelings we are then able to manage them. Being mindful will improve your relationships, help reduce stress or depression, it can even have a positive effect on physical problems like chronic pain. Mindfulness involves accepting the way things are for better or worse rather than concentrating on changing them.

2. **3 good things:** be grateful, be thankful, and show appreciation. Although saying Thank You is nice being grateful is much more. Not taking things for granted while having a sense of appreciation and thankfulness. And those who are grateful and perfect "Just love it" tend to be happier, healthier, and more fulfilled. Being grateful and having a "Just Love it" attitude can help cope with stress and can even have a beneficial effect on your heart rate.

3. **Letter of thanks:** notice it, pencil it, and share it. Journaling is powerful but studies have shown expressing our gratitude to others can significantly boost our happiness. It goes without saying it has a profound effect on recipient receiving letter of thanks and help strengthen their relationships. Who doesn't appreciate a nice letter of thanks.

4. **Extra acts of kindness:** Do something for others known or unknown every day. As the saying goes:" if you want to feel good, do good". When

you choose to help others it is not only good for the recipient, it has a positive payback for your own happiness and health. When people experience kindness it also makes them kinder and as a result contagious kindness may explode. Here are just a few acts of kindness for you to consider: Give up your seat, hold the door open for someone else, give someone a hug, smile at someone, let one car in on every journey, pick up litter as you walk, offer your change to someone struggling to find the right amount, pass on a book you've enjoyed, bake something for a neighbor, donate your old things to charity, give blood, visit someone who may be lonely or sick, volunteer your time for a charity, our plan great street party.

5. **Use your strengths:** Everyone has God given talents, and everyone should share them. Using our strengths his more about focusing on things that come most naturally to us and that we love to do. Research shows using our strengths in new ways can make us happier even after just one week. Don't know what your strengths are? Considering biting your friends over in going over the following: it's hard to identify our own strengths but easy to identify the strengths of those we love. So ask your friends to list your top five strengths and you do the same for them. You'll find each of you have a signature strength. Once you've identified your strength review them. Ask the following questions about your strengths. Do I fill naturally drawn to the strength, excited, and energized. Do I feel surprised by it, is this really mean? How much do I use this strength currently, at work or at home? And last have others seen this strength in me. Every day over the next week or so try to use this strength in a new way or in a new area of your life.

6. **Look for the good in all people:** Appreciating the good things about someone important in your life is highest compliment that can be paid. Truly focusing on a partner, close friend, or family member while remembering what drew you to your partner or your friend when you first met, or the thing you really enjoy doing together, and what you really appreciate about them along with their strengths gives you an opportunity to acknowledge the things you must appreciate and share it with them.

I'd like to leave you with this one loving thought, "Breathe it All in and Love it All Out!

About the Author

Tannen Ellis-Graham: Founder of Healthy MindSet International left the corporate world to become more engaged in projects with community impact, and personal growth. Her work focuses on bringing people together. Coaching, training, and speaking for individuals, team leaders, non-profits, and organizations that desire to hire and retain a Healthy Happy workforce.

As a Coach, Positive Psychology guru, Certified DiSC and EQ-1 2.0 Training Partners, Tannen works with Executives, Hiring managers, and Entrepreneurs to insure they are Hiring Happy, Healthy, and Productive Employees, who LOVE what they do, and Keep them!

As a Speaker and Board Member of National Speakers Association Mountain West chapter, Tannen is on a mission to bring Happy back into the work place! Positive Psychology is a real science, not just a fluff word. Happy Employees stay long and produce more and that's a scientific fact!

Tannen is the former Director of Human Resources and Operations at The Loveland Living Planet Aquarium the 5th largest Aquarium in the US. She serves as a board member for the Draper City Chamber, and is a member of both SHRM and National Association of Women Business Owners (NAWBO). She enjoyed serving as the Former Chairman of the Department of Workforce Employers Compensation Appeals Board (ECAB), and is a recovering serial entrepreneur.

She lives near Snowbird, Utah with her husband Tim, Daughter Taitlynn, stepdaughter Julia; stepsons Ian and Theo, 3 cats (Gracie, Toby, Echo) and one crazy Pomeranian Shih Tzu mix named Tallulah. Skiing the greatest snow on earth during the winter and hiking and trying to golf during the summer are just a few things Tannen enjoys.

Tannen Ellis-Graham
Founder
Healthy MindSet Intl
Tannen@healthymindsetintl.com

www.ingramcontent.com/pod-product-compliance
Lightning Source LLC
Chambersburg PA
CBHW052045090426
42739CB00010B/2058